青年学者文丛

信息科学学术英语词汇手册

李佳蕾 著

北京邮电大学出版社
www.buptpress.com

内 容 简 介

《信息科学学术英语词汇手册》基于信息科学英语语料库构建学术词表,旨在帮助学生掌握信息通信专业学术英语词汇和短语。本词汇手册收录核心词汇600个,按照词频高低进行排序,其中五星词汇200个、四星词汇200个、三星词汇200个。本词汇手册计划帮助学生利用300天的时间,每天掌握2个信息通信专业词汇及其短语和用法。每个词条呈现的主要内容包括音标、词性、中文释义、短语和例句。本词汇手册有助于信息通信专业学生拓展专业学术词汇,为其学术交流和写作打下良好基础。

图书在版编目(CIP)数据

信息科学学术英语词汇手册 / 李佳蕾著. -- 北京:北京邮电大学出版社,2024.3
ISBN 978-7-5635-7174-1

Ⅰ.①信… Ⅱ.①李… Ⅲ.①信息技术-英语-词汇-手册 Ⅳ.①G202-62

中国国家版本馆 CIP 数据核字(2024)第 047227 号

策划编辑:马晓仟　　责任编辑:廖 娟　　责任校对:张会良　　封面设计:七星博纳

出版发行:北京邮电大学出版社
社　　址:北京市海淀区西土城路 10 号
邮政编码:100876
发 行 部:电话:010-62282185　传真:010-62283578
E-mail:publish@bupt.edu.cn
经　　销:各地新华书店
印　　刷:保定市中画美凯印刷有限公司
开　　本:787 mm×1 092 mm　1/16
印　　张:15
字　　数:400 千字
版　　次:2024 年 3 月第 1 版
印　　次:2024 年 3 月第 1 次印刷

ISBN 978-7-5635-7174-1　　　　　　　　　　　　　　　　　　　　定价:68.00 元

・如有印装质量问题,请与北京邮电大学出版社发行部联系・

前　言

　　学术英语词汇是衡量学生学术英语能力的重要指标，也是影响学生学术写作和学术文章发表的重要因素。West（1953）创建的通用词汇表（General Service List，GSL）划定了 2 000 个英语常用词族。Coxhead（2000）创建的学术词汇表（Academic Word List，AWL）包含了 570 个通用学术词族，涵盖了多个专业的共享高频学术词汇。按照 Nation（2016）对词汇的分类，如果学生能够熟练掌握通用词汇表、学术词汇表和至少 5% 的专业英语词汇，就能够理解本专业学术语篇中至少 95% 的内容。

　　然而，学术英语词汇的习得较为困难。一方面，大学综合英语课堂教学以通用非学术文本为主，很难全面照顾不同专业学生的学术英语词汇学习需求。例如，学生在综合英语课堂上能够熟练掌握基础高频词汇的用法，然而对所学专业学术英语词汇的意义和用法却不够熟悉。另一方面，现有专业英语词典篇幅过长，较为枯燥，且脱离语境，不太适合学生专业英语词汇的习得。

　　《信息科学学术英语词汇手册》基于信息科学英语语料库构建学术词表，以专业知识为依托，探索语言的规律和应用。通过有针对性的训练，帮助学生掌握信息通信专业学术英语词汇和短语，尽快融入信息科学领域学术话语共同体，更顺利地进行学术写作与交流。同时，教师还可以对学术词汇表进行加工，提取本词汇表中的语言实例设计教学练习和活动，帮助学生巩固所学知识，最终使其熟练掌握信息科学领域的专业词汇。

　　本书为中央高校基本科研业务费专项资金资助项目，项目名称为"语料库驱动的大学英语听说教材与真实语言使用差异研究"，项目编号为 2023RC41。

作　者

编写说明

《信息科学学术英语词汇手册》是一本基于 InfoDEAP 信息科学（计算机科学）学术英语语料库编写的词汇手册，旨在帮助学生积累信息科学专业词汇和短语，培养学生的专业英语能力，为其学术阅读、写作和交流打下坚实的基础。本词汇手册依据词汇在语料库中出现的频率从高到低进行排序，不仅涵盖了信息科学领域的专业词汇，还给出了一些常见词汇在信息科学领域的特殊含义；不仅满足了信息科学相关专业学生的基本文献阅读和写作需要，还为信息科学学术英语教学和教材编写提供了依据。

InfoDEAP 信息科学（计算机科学）学术英语语料库

InfoDEAP 信息科学（计算机科学）学术英语语料库是 DEAP（Database of English for Academic Purposes）学术英语语料库的一个分支，主要由大连外国语大学邓耀臣教授负责建设。DEAP 学术英语语料库涵盖 20 余个学科分支，以《学位授予和人才培养一级学科简介（2013 年）》为基准划分，总库容达 1.2 亿词次。DEAP 学术英语语料库项目于 2016 年启动，项目主要牵头成员包括许家金教授、梁茂成教授、李文中教授和熊文新教授。本词汇手册中使用到的 InfoDEAP 信息科学（计算机科学）学术英语语料库总计 1 278 篇文章，总库容达 5 274 963 词次，单篇文章平均 4 128 词次。

选词依据

1. 最低频率：本词汇手册中所选词条在 InfoDEAP 信息科学（计算机科学）学术英语语料库中出现的最低频率为 150。为了确定选词频率，本词汇手册参考了 Coxhead（2000）在建设学术英语词汇表（Academic Word List，AWL）时的选词频率，即找出频率为 100 的词族，需要 350 万词的语料库。经过计算，对于库容超过 500 万词的 InfoDEAP 信息科学（计算机科学）学术英语语料库，选词频率最终确定为 150。

2. 学科词汇：本词汇手册关注所选词汇在信息科学中的特定含义。此前学科词汇表为了最大限度地反映专业词汇的用法，排除了通用词汇表（General Service List，GSL）中的词汇。然而，通用词汇表中的一些词汇（如"bug"和"tree"）在信息科学中的特殊含义不容忽视。"bug"在通用英语中最常见的含义为"小昆虫、虫子"，而在信息科学中多指"机器故障"或"程序错误"；"tree"在通用英语中最常见的含义为"树木"，而在信息科学中多指"树形结构"。因此，本词汇手册并没有完全将通用词汇表中的词汇排除在外，而是参考《牛津英汉双解计算机词典》和《牛津数学词典》编写信息科学词汇表，找出不同词汇在信息科学中的含义。

3. 标明词性：本词汇手册标明了不同词汇的词性。例如，对于"set"一词，我们对其名词含义"集合""系"和动词含义"设置"进行了区分。

4. 词形还原：本词汇手册在制作词汇表时采用的是词形还原形式（Lemma）而非词族（Word Family）。词形还原指的是去掉单词的词缀，提取主干部分，同时标明词汇的具体词性。词族包含了词汇的所有曲折形式，并不强调词性的作用。然而，词性对于学术英语词汇表至关重要。例如，"write"在语言学中多指"学术写作"，而在信息科学中多为"写入"的含义。本词汇手册利用语料库工具 LancsBox（Brezina et al.，2015）进行分词、词性标注、词形还原以及词表的制作和频率筛选。

5. 词汇分布：为确保所选词汇在 InfoDEAP 信息科学（计算机科学）学术英语语料库中均匀分布，本词汇手册参考了 Gardner 和 Davies（2014）以及 Lei 和 Liu（2016）的做法，选择 Juilland's D 作为衡量词汇分布的指标，并规定本词汇手册中 Juilland's D 的取值不得小于 0.5。

6. 排除词汇：本词汇手册参考了 Nation（2016）的做法，排除了专有名词、首字母缩略词、计量单位、数字和公式符号。

内容构成

本词汇手册收录核心词汇 600 个，按照词频高低进行排序，其中五星词汇 200 个，四星词汇 200 个，三星词汇 200 个。本词汇手册计划帮助学生利用 300 天的时间，每天掌握 2 个信息通信专业词汇及其短语和用法。每个词条呈现的主要内容包括音标、词性、中文释义、短语和例句。由于单词词义难以独立确定，因此本词汇手册以短语和例句的形式共同呈现信息科学核心词汇的含义。

目 录

第一部分　五星词汇 …………………………………………………………… 1

第二部分　四星词汇 …………………………………………………………… 75

第三部分　三星词汇 …………………………………………………………… 149

总词汇表 ………………………………………………………………………… 224

参考文献 ………………………………………………………………………… 232

第一部分
五星词汇

Day 1

model

/ˈmɒdl/ n. 模型

data **model**	数据模型
conceptual **model**	概念模型
environmental **model**	环境模型
simulation **model**	模拟模型
regression **model**	回归模型

These features ensure a high level of correspondence between the underlying conceptual model and users' mental model, enabling the user to concentrate on their decision-making process rather than add to their cognitive load.
这些特征确保潜在的概念模型和用户的心智模型之间存在较强的相关关系,确保用户能够关注决策过程而增加非认知负荷。

system

/ˈsɪstəm/ n. 系统

information **system**	信息系统
operating **system**	操作系统
software **system**	软件系统
management **system**	管理系统
linear **system**	线性系统

Each of these algorithms preserves a particular property of a given information system.
其中每一个算法都保留了某个信息系统的特定特征。

Day 2

data / datum

/ˈdeɪtə/
/ˈdeɪtəm/ n. 数据

data storage	数据存储
data generation	数据生成
data aggregation	数据聚合
data migration	数据迁移
data property	数据属性

Data mining was performed by downloading all articles published in 2008 for each journal in HTML format.
我们将2008年每一期刊中的所有文章下载保存为HTML格式进行数据挖掘。

algorithm

/ˈælgərɪðəm/ *n.* 算法

clustering **algorithm**	聚类算法
routing **algorithm**	路由算法
k-means **algorithm**	*k* 均值算法
greedy **algorithm**	贪婪算法

Section 6 describes the clustering algorithms used in the study.
第六节描述了本研究中用到的聚类算法。

Day 3

network

/ˈnetwɜːk/ *n.* 网络

network traffic	网络流量
network resources	网络资源
network graph	网络图表
network coding	网络编码
network security	网络安全

In this case, the workload imbalance is nearly constant and no network traffic occurs.
在这种情况下,工作量失衡持续存在,不会出现网络流量。

set

/set/ *n.* 集合;系

training **set**	训练集
test **set**	测试集
parameter **set**	参数集
finite **set**	有限集
feature **set**	特征集

The narrow width of the confidence interval of the proposed algorithm implies that the performance of the proposed algorithm is less affected by changes in the training sets.
上述提出算法中置信区间中较窄的宽度表明,这一算法受训练集变化的影响较小。

Day 4

node
/nəʊd/ *n.* 节点

leaf **node**	叶节点
node name	节点名
node address	节点地址
grid **node**	网格节点
node type	节点类型

As the search depth increases, the relevance of the evaluation made at the leaf nodes decreases.
随着搜索深度增加,叶节点评价关联度减弱。

process
/ˈprəʊses/ *n.* (任务)处理过程

process quality	过程质量
process improvement	流程改进
process communication	进程通信
engineering **process**	工程过程
diffusion **process**	扩散过程

Previous work has focused heavily on studying communication patterns of software teams to explore and explain the knowledge diffusion process.
此前工作一直十分关注研究软件团队的交际模式来探索和解释知识传播过程。

Day 5

base

/beɪs/ *v.* 以……为基础

base on	以……为基础
base upon	以……为基础

In order to compare the different strategies, we base our simulations on the following scenario.
为了比较不同的策略,我们将以下面的情形作为模拟基准。

function

/'fʌŋkʃn/ *n.* 函数;子程序

distribution function	分布函数
utility function	效用函数
density function	密度函数
value function	价值函数
fitness function	适应度函数

As there was a large amount of training data available, the parameter values of each distribution function were determined by maximum likelihood estimation.
鉴于我们有大量训练数据,每一分布函数的参数价值通过最大似然估计确定。

Day 6

security

/sɪˈkjʊərəti/ *n.* 安全

security awareness	安全意识
security requirement	安全性要求
security breaches	安全漏洞
security measure	安全措施
security rule	安全规则

The research explores factors that affect information security awareness of staff.
本研究探索了影响员工信息安全意识的因素。

application

/ˌæplɪˈkeɪʃn/ n. 应用；应用程序

scientific **application**	科学应用
application layer	应用层
application logic	应用逻辑
application testing	应用测试
application programming	应用程序编辑

Social networks provide modules and Application Programming Interfaces (APIs) that allow developers to extract information from a user's profile with his or her permission.
社会网络提供了组件和应用程序编辑界面，使得开发人员能够在用户允许的情况下从用户概貌中提取信息。

Day 7

level

/ˈlevl/ n. 级别；水平；层次

security **level**	安全级别
noise **level**	噪声水平
confidence **level**	置信水平
abstraction **level**	抽象层次
significance **level**	显著性水平

This test is performed at the 95% significance level.
本测试的显著性水平为95%。

type

/taɪp/ n. 类型

entity **type**	实体类型
type hierarchy	类型层次结构
type theory	类型论

We measure the degree of similarity by taking the intersection between the paths from the root of the type hierarchy.
我们通过类型层次结构路径交叉点衡量相似性。

Day 8

parameter

/pəˈræmɪtə(r)/ *n.* 参数；变量

parameter value	参数值
parameter space	参数空间
parameter settings	参数设置
parameter sensitivity	参数灵敏度

It is interesting to note that there is no link between parameter sensitivity and maximum calibration performance.
有趣的是，参数敏感性和最大校准性能之间并没有联系。

set

/set/ *v.* 设置

set the password	设置密码
set the boundary	设置界限
set the value	设置取值
set the aggregation function	设置集合函数

We set the value as small as possible.
我们尽可能把数值设置得小一些。

Day 9

table

/ˈteɪbl/ *n.* 表

routing **table**	路由表
hash **table**	哈希表
neighbor **table**	邻居表,邻接表
probability **table**	概率表

The path bandwidth for each of the nodes in the routing table is calculated.
我们计算了路由表中每个节点的路径带宽。

path

/pɑːθ/ *n.* 路径;指令序列;访问路径

shortest **path**	最短路径
overlay **path**	重叠通路
optimal **path**	最优路径
network **path**	网络路径
backup **path**	备份路径,后备路径

In addition to mean backup path length, we also collected statistics on the maximum backup path length in each graph.
除了平均备份路径长度,我们同时收集了每个图表中的最大备份路径长度。

Day 10

image

/ˈɪmɪdʒ/ *n.* 图片;影像

face **image**	人脸图像
original **image**	原始图像
document **image**	文档图像
facial **image**	人脸图像
medical **image**	医学影像

A novel restoration and reconstruction method for document images is introduced.
我们引入了一个全新的文档图像恢复和重构方法。

query

/ˈkwɪəri/ *n.* 查询

query execution	查询执行
query expansion	查询扩展
structured query language	结构化查询语言
query result	查询结果
query pattern	查询模式

Structured Query Language (SQL) is a standard interactive language used with relational databases.
结构化查询语言是与关系数据库一同应用的一种标准互动型语言。

Day 11

domain

/dəˈmeɪn/ n. 控制区域；函数域；范围

application domain	应用领域
computational domain	计算域
reference domain	参考域
spatial domain	空间域
time domain	时间域

Variations in text and background intensity over the document image domain can be very local.
文档图像域文本和背景强度差异可能是局部的。

software

/ˈsɒftweə(r)/ n. 软件

scientific software	科学软件
empirical software	经验软件
commercial software	商业软件
open-source software	开源软件
application software	应用软件

Section 3 provides more details about these characteristics of scientific software.
第三节描述了这些科学软件的更多细节特征。

Day 12

search
/sɜːtʃ/ *n.* 检索；查找

search engine	搜索引擎
search process	搜索过程
search algorithm	搜索算法
search method	搜索法
search tree	搜索树

Turn-based games naturally impose a rigid structure on search trees.
回合制游戏对搜索树有严格的结构要求。

variable
/ˈveəriəbl/ *n.* 变量；变量名称

random variable	随机变量
state variable	状态变量
dependent variable	因变量
independent variable	自变量
design variable	设计参数；设计变量

We collected dependent variable data for whether participants had written critical/negative comments in blogs or other social media websites.
我们收集了因变量数据，考察参与者是否在博客或其他社会媒体网站上给出过批评或者负面评价。

Day 13

element
/ˈelɪmənt/ *n.* 部件；元件；元素

| finite element | 有限元 |
| tetrahedral element | 四面体元 |

hexahedral **element**	六面体元
diagonal **element**	对角元素
element space	元素空间

Many algorithms are now available for fast and accurate automatic mesh generation using tetrahedral elements.
借助四面体元,许多算法现在可以实现快速、准确的自动网格生成。

graph

/grɑːf/ *n.* 图;图解

intersection **graph**	交集图
knowledge **graph**	知识图谱
acyclic **graph**	无环图
undirected **graph**	无向图
weighted **graph**	加权图;带权图

We hence complete the weighted graph outlined above by the use of soft links.
因此,我们采用软链接完成了上面的加权图。

Day 14

class

/klɑːs/ *n.* 类

class label	类标签
class hierarchy	类层次结构
class imbalance	类别不平衡
class name	类名
class expression	类表达式

By contrast, the current approach does not require class labels on the database, and thus can be used when class membership information is not available.
相反,现有方法并不需要数据库中的类标签,即使没有类成员信息也可以使用。

simulation

/ˌsɪmjuˈleɪʃn/ *n.* 模拟;仿造物

Monte-Carlo **simulation**	蒙特卡罗模拟
numerical simulation	数值模拟
dynamics **simulation**	动力学仿真
simulation time	模拟时间
simulation experiment	模拟实验；仿真实验

For each case that we investigate, we compare our results with those obtained from simulation experiments.
对于我们调查的每一个案例，我们将结果与仿真实验进行对比。

Day 15

knowledge
/ˈnɒlɪdʒ/ *n.* 知识

knowledge base	知识库
knowledge sharing	知识共享
knowledge representation	知识表示
knowledge management	知识管理
knowledge diffusion	知识扩散

Here we are concerned with the interface between the knowledge base and its user, which might be a person or an application program.
这里我们关注的是知识库和用户之间的界面，可能是一个人或一个应用项目。

source
/sɔːs/ *n.* 源

source code	源代码
source management	资源管理
source software	源代码软件
source data	源数据
source image	源图像

We developed our own client applications and selected open source software to secure their connections.
我们研发了自己的客户应用并选择开源软件保证它们连接的稳定性。

Day 16

task

/tɑːsk/ *n.* 处理;作业

classification **task**	分类任务
task performance	任务表现;工作效能
task completion	任务完成
task allocation	任务分配

Throughout our experiments, we focus on how these dimensions interact to affect task performance.
通过我们的实验,我们关注这些维度如何相互作用影响任务表现。

pattern

/ˈpætn/ *n.* 模式;方案

pattern recognition	模式识别
pattern classification	模式分类
pattern matching	模式匹配
pattern mining	模式挖掘;模式发掘
pattern vector	模式矢量

This technique is similar to the one found in pattern recognition.
这一技术与模式识别十分相似。

Day 17

web

/web/ *n.* 网

web service	网络服务
web search	网络搜索
web application	网络应用

web technology	网络技术
web science	网络科学

In this paper a number of web services are introduced.
本文介绍了大量网络服务。

resource

/rɪˈsɔːs/ *n.* 资源

resource service	资源服务
resource usage	资源利用；资源使用
resource provision	资源供应
computing resource	计算资源
network resource	网络资源

The emergence of open grid infrastructures has enabled scientists to exploit unprecedented computing resources for data-intensive research.
开放网格服务基础设施的涌现使科学家们可以利用前所未有的计算资源进行数据密集型研究。

Day 18

constraint

/kənˈstreɪnt/ *n.* 受限；约束

constraint satisfaction	受限满足
constraint function	约束函数
constraint programming	约束规划

Section 8.1 provides a discussion of work on distributed constraint satisfaction.
8.1小节讨论了分布式约束满足相关研究。

distribution

/ˌdɪstrɪˈbjuːʃn/ *n.* 分布

probability distribution	概率分布
normal distribution	正态分布
posterior distribution	后验分布

spatial **distribution**	空间分布
cumulative **distribution**	累积分布

The samples of one class follows a normal distribution, while the samples of the other class form two clusters.
一个班级的样本符合正态分布,而另一个班级的样本形成了两个聚类。

Day 19

input

/ˈɪnpʊt/ *n.* 输入

input parameter	输入参数
input variable	输入变量;输入值
input space	输入空间
input validation	输入验证
input message	输入信息

Each input parameter can have a different range and interval values.
每一个输入参数的范围和间隔值都可能不同。

framework

/ˈfreɪmwɜːk/ *n.* 构架;结构

security **framework**	安全框架
evaluation **framework**	评价框架
lightweight **framework**	轻量级框架
simulation **framework**	模拟框架
assessment **framework**	评估框架

In the next section the cases are applied to the conceptual framework.
下一节中所有的案例将用于概念框架。

Day 20

instance
/ˈɪnstəns/ *n.* 事例；示例；例化

instance type	实例类型
instance data	实例数据；实例资料
database **instance**	数据库实例

This instance data describes the protein name.
这一实例数据描述了蛋白质名称。

structure
/ˈstrʌktʃə(r)/ *n.* 结构；数据关系；数据结构

reward **structure**	酬偿结构；奖励结构；利润构成
tree **structure**	树状结构
syntactic **structure**	句法结构
structure support	结构支撑
structure component	结构成分

In order to take advantage of the above benefits, in this study we will connect VPN endpoints using a tree structure.
为了利用上述优势，本研究中我们用一个树状结构把VPN端点连接在一起。

Day 21

error
/ˈerə(r)/ 错误；差错；失误

error rate	错误率
error tolerance	容错；误差宽容度
error bar	误差线
error correction	错误纠正
error estimate	误差估计；误差估计值

The error bars represent the standard error in the mean.
误差线展示了平均值中的标准误差。

probability

/ˌprɒbəˈbɪləti/ *n.* 概率

probability distribution	概率分布
probability density	概率密度
probability measure	概率测度
probability ratio	概率比
conditional **probability**	条件概率

A Probability Density Function (PDF) states the probability for every number of positive elements in the sample.
概率密度函数描述了样本中的每一个积极元素的概率。

Day 22

code

/kəʊd/ *n.* 代码

function **code**	功能代码
model **code**	型号代码
dynamics **code**	动态验证码
protection **code**	保护码
computer **code**	计算机代码

The complete computer code of the proposed methodology and metadata on the program structure are provided as supplementary files.
提出方法的完整计算机代码和项目结构的元数据作为补充文件出现。

evaluation

/ɪˌvæljuˈeɪʃn/ *n.* 评价

performance **evaluation**	绩效评估
function **evaluation**	函数求值；功能评价
experimental **evaluation**	实验评价

| quantitative **evaluation** | 量化评价 |
| quality **evaluation** | 质量评价 |

We successfully validate the effectiveness of our best methods in a real-world performance evaluation of multicast routing.
我们成功验证了我们的最佳方法在现实世界多址通信路径选择绩效评估中的有效性。

Day 23

model

/ˈmɒdl/ v. (用计算机)做出(情景、事件)的模型

| **model** a conversation | 模拟对话 |
| **model** each single dialogue | 模拟每一个单一对话 |

We also show how these aspects can be exploited to model each single dialogue participant.
我们同样展示出如何利用这些方面模拟每一个单一对话参与者。

compute

/kəmˈpjuːt/ v. 计算；估算

compute similarity	计算相似性
compute resources	计算资源
compute node	计算节点
compute machine	计算机器

However, they only consider the use of compute machines and private/public cloud allocation.
然而，他们只考虑到计算机的使用和私人/公共云分配。

Day 24

definition

/ˌdefɪˈnɪʃn/ n. 定义

formal definition	正式定义
operational definition	操作性定义
precise definition	精确定义
standard definition	标准定义
language definition	语言定义

This section describes the operational definition.
这一节描述了操作性定义。

edge

/edʒ/ n. 边；边缘；界限

edge weight	边权
edge detection	边缘检测

This can be done, for instance, by defining a cost function that calculates the average edge weight.
例如,这可以通过定义成本函数计算边权实现。

Day 25

implementation

/ˌɪmplɪmenˈteɪʃn/ v. 执行

model implementation	模型实现
practical implementation	实际执行；实际运用
software implementation	软件实现
system implementation	系统实施

Second, the actual performance of the parallel implementation is assessed by measuring the speed-up in a series of benchmark tests.
其次,并行执行的实际表现通过衡量一系列基准测试中的加速展现。

object

/ˈɒbdʒɪkt/ n. 对象

physical **object**	物体
object code	目标码
object-oriented programming	面向对象程序设计
object-oriented design	面向对象设计
object-oriented software	面向对象软件

Most distributed system applications are created using object-oriented programming language.
多数分布式系统应用的设计使用了面向对象程序设计语言。

Day 26

ontology

/ɒnˈtɒlədʒi/ *n.* 本体论

ontology engineering	本体论工程
ontology matching	本体匹配
ontology learning	本体学习
ontology language	本体论语言
domain **ontology**	领域本体

These studies can be roughly divided into three areas: (i) ontology learning from text, (ii) interactive ontology learning, (iii) concept learning.
这些研究可以粗略分为三个领域:(i) 文本本体学习;(ii) 互动本体学习;(iii) 概念学习。

traffic

/ˈtræfɪk/ *n.* 通信(量)

network **traffic**	网络流量
data **traffic**	数据流量
traffic matrix	通信量矩阵
traffic analysis	流量分析
traffic capacity	(传输线的)通话能力

For example, in order to minimize network traffic, the network administrator may require the host device to authenticate user samples.
例如,为了把网络流量降到最低,网络管理员可能会要求主机设备验证用户样本。

Day 27

sequence
/ˈsiːkwəns/ *n.* 序列

sequence diagram	时序图
sequence number	序列号
sequence length	序列长度
sequence analysis	序列分析
sequence alignment	序列比对

Features can be constructed manually, or by using data mining methods such as sequence analysis.
我们可以手动构建特征,或者使用序列分析这样的数据挖掘方法。

link
/lɪŋk/ *n.* 连接;指针连接;网节

link quality	环节质量;链路质量
link failure	链路故障
link capacity	链路容量
link flow	链接流
link state	链路状态

This will allow a practical and realistic approach for the link quality evaluation purpose.
这将使我们为链路质量评价找到实际、现实的方法。

Day 28

form
/fɔːm/ *n.* 版面;格式

propositional form	命题形式
characteristic form	特征形式
representation form	表现形式

functional **form**	函数形式
bilinear **form**	双线性型

The detailed functional form is complicated.
详细的函数形式是复杂的。

tree

/triː/ *n.* 目录树;树形表;树形结构

spanning **tree**	生成树
decision **tree**	决策树
event **tree**	事件树
definition **tree**	定义树
execution **tree**	执行树

The decision tree above is also more space efficient than a cache for the same data.
对于同样的数据来说,上述决策树比高速缓存更加节省空间。

Day 29

message

/ˈmesɪdʒ/ *n.* 消息;报文;数据包;文件传输格式;对象

output **message**	输出信息;输出消息
update **message**	更新消息
probe **message**	探测消息
nested **message**	嵌套的消息
spam **message**	垃圾信息

Input message is a simple XML message.
输入消息是一个简单的 XML 消息。

vector

/ˈvektə(r)/ *n.* 向量

support **vector** machine	支持向量机
feature **vector**	特征向量

numerical **vector**	数字向量
input **vector**	输入矢量
velocity **vector**	速度矢量

Support Vector Machine (SVM) is a state-of-the-art supervised learning algorithm commonly used in many applications for both regression and classification purpose.
支持向量机是一种先进的监督学习算法,常见于许多回归和分类应用中。

Day 30

representation
/ˌreprɪzenˈteɪʃn/ *n.* 表示

knowledge **representation**	知识表示
vector **representation**	矢量表示法
graphical **representation**	图形表示
resource **representation**	资源表示
matrix **representation**	矩阵表示

A common concept in knowledge representation is to define the meaning of a term not through explicit definitions in the language, but by attaching a piece of code to be executed for computing the meaning of the term.
这是知识表示中一个常见概念,即不通过语言中的显定义界定术语的含义,而是通过执行代码运算找出术语的含义。

interaction
/ˌɪntərˈækʃn/ *n.* 相互作用

feature **interaction**	特征交互;特征相互作用
fluid-structure **interaction**	流体结构相互作用
interaction effect	交互作用
interaction information	互动信息
interaction protocol	交互协议

We rely entirely on the context provided by the interaction protocol and the concrete interaction states.
我们完全依赖交互协议提供的情境和具体的交互状态。

Day 31

select

/sɪˈlekt/ *v.* 选取;选择

select the best solution	选取最佳方案
select the appropriate level	选取恰当的水平
select the appropriate member	选取恰当的成员
select the most salient direction	选取最突出的方向
select the simulation	选择模拟

We then use a random algorithm to select the appropriate members.
接着,我们使用随机算法选择恰当的成员。

range

/reɪndʒ/ *n.* 域;范围

broad **range**	广泛范围
range multiplier	扩程器,量程扩大器
range constraint	范围约束
range parameter	范围参数

Results from early experiments carried out over the past two years indicate that a broad range of researchers are able to conduct investigations.
过去两年的早期实验结果显示,大量研究人员可以开展调查。

Day 32

matrix

/ˈmeɪtrɪks/ *n.* 矩阵

covariance **matrix**	协方差矩阵
adjacency **matrix**	邻接矩阵
identity **matrix**	单位矩阵

stiffness **matrix**	刚度矩阵
affinity **matrix**	亲和矩阵

If the size of covariance matrix is large then finding the eigenvectors might be difficult.
如果协方差矩阵很大,那么寻找特征向量可能十分困难。

cluster

/ˈklʌstə(r)/ *n.* 聚类

cluster analysis	聚类分析
cluster center	簇中心;聚类中心
cluster network	群聚网络
hierarchical **cluster**	层次聚类
index **cluster**	索引集群

Cluster analysis, also known as unsupervised data classification, is an important subject in data mining.
聚类分析,又称无监督数据分类,是数据挖掘中的重要议题。

Day 33

language

/ˈlæŋgwɪdʒ/ *n.* 计算机语言

language processing	语言处理
language model	语言模型
language expression	语言表达
language generation	语言生成
language definition	语言定义

I will not address language generation, conceptual learning, language learning, or the semantics of social or abstract domains.
我并不会谈及语言生成、概念学习、语言学习或是社会和抽象领域的语义学。

classification

/ˌklæsɪfɪˈkeɪʃn/ *n.* 分类

pattern **classification**	模式分类
binary **classification**	二元分类
data **classification**	数据分类
vehicle **classification**	车型分类
supervised **classification**	有监督分类

The actual performance of different techniques varies considerably with the uniqueness and sophistication of the pattern classification engine.
不同策略的实际表现与模式分类引擎的独特性和复杂性差异很大。

Day 34

location

/ləʊˈkeɪʃn/ *n.* 定位

geographic **location**	地理位置
physical **location**	实际位置
vehicle **location**	车辆定位
sampling **location**	采样地点
multiple **location**	多个位置

Users can also view real-time vehicle location by tapping on its icon.
用户通过图标查看车辆实时定位。

scheme

/skiːm/ *n.* 计划；方案

classification **scheme**	分类方案
numerical **scheme**	数值化方案
authentication **scheme**	认证方案；验证方案
protection **scheme**	保护方案
routing **scheme**	路由选择方案；布线图

The main limitation of these taxonomies is the narrowness of their classification schemes.
这些分类学的主要局限是它们的分类方案范围较窄。

Day 35

access

/ˈækses/ n. 读写数据;存取权;访问

wireless access	无线访问
network access	网络访问
physical access	物理访问
remote access	远程访问
spectrum access	频谱访问

To accomplish a complete distributed surveillance system there needs to be a remote access framework.
想要完成一套完整的分布监测体系,我们需要远程访问框架。

database

/ˈdeɪtəbeɪs/ n. 数据库

relational database	关系型数据库
speech database	语音数据库
image database	图像数据库
training database	训练数据库
local database	本地数据库

There should be some criteria that can be used to judge how well a certain emotional database simulates a real-world environment.
判定特定情感数据库模拟真实环境情况应有一些标准。

Day 36

program

/ˈprəʊɡræm/ n. 程序

program comprehension	程式理解,程序理解
program behavior	程序动作

program execution	程序执行
program board	程序控制盘
program version	程序版本

The program boundary was also crossed in negotiations on choice of methodology.
项目边界同样根据选择的方法进行交叉谈判。

packet

/ˈpækɪt/ n. 分组；包

data packet	数据包
routing packet	路由数据包
network packet	网络数据包
virtual packet	虚拟包

Using this setup, we collected many data packets.
借助这一设置，我们收集了许多数据包。

Day 37

document

/ˈdɒkjumənt/ n. 文件

document collection	文档收集
document image	文档图像
document retrieval	文档检索
document browsing	文档浏览

Before an LDA analysis can be performed on the document collection using the tool, the following parameters must be set.
在使用工具对文档收集进行线性判别分析之前，必须设置以下参数。

operation

/ˌɒpəˈreɪʃn/ n. 操作；运算指令；运算程序

normal **operation**	正常操作
basic **operation**	基本操作
swap **operation**	交换操作

We define normal operation to be the state of the network when there are no adverse conditions present.
如果没有相反的条件，我们即把网络状态定义为正常操作。

Day 38

entity

/ˈentəti/ *n.* 实体

entity recognition	实体识别，实体辨认
entity type	实体类型
name **entity** recognition	命名实体识别

The authors investigate the impact of several text preprocessing steps: language identification, tokenization, POS tagging and named entity recognition.
作者考察了多个文本预处理步骤的影响：语言识别、分词、词性标注和命名实体识别。

environment

/ɪnˈvaɪrənmənt/ *n.* 环境

computing **environment**	计算环境
development **environment**	开发环境

This approach to request handling works nicely in a cloud computing environment.
这种处理请求的方法在云计算环境中表现很出色。

Day 39

measure

/ˈmeʒə(r)/ *v.* 度量

measure the similarity	度量相似性
measure the performance	度量表现
measure the effectiveness	度量有效性
measure the impact	度量影响
measure the accuracy	度量准确性

To measure the effectiveness of the approach, we conducted experiments.
为了度量方法的有效性,我们进行了试验。

optimal

/ˈɒptɪməl/ *adj.* 最优的

optimal solution	最优解决方案
optimal value	最优值
optimal path	最优路径
optimal design	最优设计
optimal response	最佳回应

This ensures that the optimal solution will not be missed.
这保证我们不会错过最优解决方案。

Day 40

equation

/ɪˈkweɪʒn/ *n.* 方程式

Fokker-Planck equation	福克尔-普朗克方程
differential equation	微分方程
sine-Gordon equation	正弦戈登方程
momentum equation	动量方程
matrix equation	矩阵方程

Recent work has shown that the direct solution of the Fokker – Planck equation can be much more efficient than stochastic methods in the case of homogeneous flows.
近期研究已经表明,就均匀流而言,福克尔-普朗克方程的直接解决方案可能比随机方法更有效。

accuracy

/ˈækjərəsi/ *n.* 精确度

classification **accuracy**	分类精度
overall **accuracy**	整体准确度
high **accuracy**	高精度
recognition **accuracy**	识别准确度
detection **accuracy**	探测精度

As expected, at high noise levels, the classification accuracy decreases as the signal quality degrades.
正如预期的那样,当噪声处于较高水平时,随着信号质量的下降,分类准确度会降低。

Day 41

technology

/tekˈnɒlədʒi/ *n.* 技术

information **technology**	信息技术
web **technology**	网络技术
semantic **technology**	语义技术
security **technology**	安全技术
consumption **technology**	消费技术

Smaller organizations spend on average nearly 20% of their overall information technology budgets on security-related products.
小型机构在安全产品上的信息技术预算平均占到了总预算的20%。

address

/əˈdres/ *v.* 寻址;解决问题

address the problem	解决问题
address the issue	解决问题

In this paper, we address the problem of classification of ground vehicles.
本文中,我们解决了陆上车辆的分类问题。

Day 42

device
/dɪˈvaɪs/ *n.* 设备；设备驱动程序

device surveillance	设备监控
device memory	设备内存
device control	设备控制

The device surveillance monitors the device's traffic.
设备监控检测了设备的通信量。

detection
/dɪˈtekʃn/ *n.* 检测

intrusion **detection**	入侵检测
fault **detection**	故障检测
outlier **detection**	离群点检测
edge **detection**	边缘检测
hotspot **detection**	热点检测

These well-known intrusion detection techniques have their own strengths and weaknesses.
这些著名的入侵检测技术有各自的优势和劣势。

Day 43

behavior / behaviour
/bɪˈheɪvjə(r)/ *n.* 行为

behavior profiling	行为分析
behavior characteristics	行为特征
behavior model	行为模型

The result of using behaviour profiling to classify users is shown in Table 5.
使用行为分析法对用户进行分类的结果详见表 5。

complexity

/kəmˈpleksəti/ *n.* 复杂度;复杂性

computational **complexity**	计算复杂度
space **complexity**	空间复杂度
code **complexity**	代码复杂性
cyclomatic **complexity**	圈复杂度
exponential **complexity**	指数复杂性

We conclude this section by briefly considering the computational complexity of the main decision questions.
本章结束时,我们简要考虑了主要决策问题中的计算复杂度。

Day 44

output

/ˈaʊtpʊt/ *n.* 输出

output data	输出数据
output message	输出信息
output layer	输出层
output variable	输出变量
output variance	输出方差

We can combine together the output of all the components of the output layer.
我们可以把输出层的所有成分合并在一起。

semantic

/sɪˈmæntɪk/ *adj.* 语义

semantic web	语义网
semantic analysis	语义分析
semantic description	语义描述
semantic annotation	语义标注
semantic processing	语义处理

Semantic Web (SW) research has produced a substantial body of work focused on providing

the essential language and tooling support to build conceptual models.
语义网研究中大量作品聚焦为搭建概念模型提供关键语言和工具支持。

Day 45

protocol
/ˈprəʊtəkɒl/ *n.* 协议

protocol model	协议模型
transfer **protocol**	传送协议
transport **protocol**	传输协议
security **protocol**	安全协议
communication **protocol**	通信协议

Recognizing the dangers in sending confidential information over an inherently insecure media, a number of secure data transport protocols have emerged.
人们意识到通过本质上不稳定的媒体传输秘密信息存在危险,因而设计了一系列稳定的数据传输协议。

computational
/ˌkɒmpjuˈteɪʃənl/ *adj.* 计算的

computational cost	计算成本
computational efficiency	计算效率
computational time	计算时间
computational effort	计算量
computational domain	计算域

There is, not surprisingly, a trade-off between computational efficiency and cost of long-range connections.
意料之中的是,计算效率和远程连接成本之间需要达到平衡。

Day 46

degree
/dɪˈgriː/ *n.* 度;深度;次数

degree of freedom	自由度
degree of confidence	置信度
degree of similarity	相似程度,贴近度
degree of uncertainty	不确定性程度
degree of correlation	相关程度

As a consequence a new degree of freedom is enjoyed allowing them to pose new kinds of queries that they were interested in.
因此,新的自由度使得他们能够展开感兴趣的全新检索。

accord

/əˈkɔːd/ v. 与……一致;相符合

in **accord** with the statistics	和数据一致
in **accord** well with the predictions	和预测十分一致
in **accord** with standardization procedure	和标准化流程一致
in **accord** with the structure	与结构一致
in **accord** with the system	与系统一致

The realization of the project will be in accord with the nature of the system.
项目的实现将与系统本质一致。

Day 47

construct

/kənˈstrʌkt/ v. 构想;构建

construct the local matrix	构建局部矩阵
construct the rainbow table	构建彩虹表
construct the global solution	构建全球解决方案
construct the response surface	构建响应曲面
construct the image	构建图像

It is expensive to construct the local matrix at query time.
在检索时构建局部矩阵成本很高。

global

/ˈgləʊbl/ *adj.* 全局的

global optimization	全局优化
global minimum	全局最小值
global constraint	全局约束
global virtual team	全球虚拟团队
global sensitivity	全局敏感性

This method allows for global sensitivity analysis with a higher level of computational efficiency than previous methods.
这一方法可以帮助我们实现全局敏感性分析,计算效率比以往的方法更高。

Day 48

dataset

/ˈdeɪtəset/ *n.* 数据集

real-world **dataset**	真实数据集
synthetic **dataset**	合成数据集
test **dataset**	测试数据集
training **dataset**	训练数据集
dataset research	数据集研究

The machine learning algorithm is trained multiple times on the training dataset.
机器学习算法在训练数据集上经过多次训练。

grid

/grɪd/ *n.* 网格

Cartesian **grid**	笛卡儿网格
power **grid**	电网
smart **grid**	智能电网
computational **grid**	计算网格
grid point	网格点

Many systems can be at risk from cyber warfare, including critical national infrastructure such as the power grid and transportation network.
许多系统都可能受到网络战争的威胁,包括电网和运输网络等国家基础设施。

Day 49

boundary

/ˈbaʊndri/ *n.* 边界

boundary condition	边界条件
boundary spanner	边界跨越者
periodic **boundary**	周期边界
decision **boundary**	决策边界
outflow **boundary**	外流边界,出流边界;外缘

We impose periodic boundary conditions in all spatial directions.
我们给所有的空间方向添加了周期边界条件。

standard

/ˈstændəd/ *adj.* 标准的

standard deviation	标准差
standard approach	标准方法
standard error	标准误差
standard implementation	标准实现
standard regression	标准回归

Error bars show the standard error.
误差线展示了标准误差。

Day 50

procedure

/prəˈsiːdʒə(r)/ *n.* 程序

solution **procedure**	解决程序
search **procedure**	搜查程序
testing **procedure**	测试程序
selection **procedure**	选拔程序
experimental **procedure**	实验程序

We follow the same experimental procedure as described in the previous section.
我们遵循了与前一章节中相同的实验程序。

list

/lɪst/ *n.* 列表

reference **list**	参考文献列表
exhaustive **list**	详细清单
drop-down **list**	下拉列表
adjacency **list**	邻接表
feature **list**	特征表

The structure is displayed as a tree that shows dimensions, attributes and measures, as well as their ranges, code lists.
该结构为树形，展示了维度、属性、措施、范围和代码列表。

Day 51

server

/ˈsɜːvə(r)/ *n.* 服务器

web **server**	网络服务器
application **server**	应用服务器
physical **server**	物理服务器
virtual **server**	虚拟服务器
mail **server**	邮件服务器

Our experiment employs three physical servers.
我们的实验采用了三个物理服务器。

key

/kiː/ *adj.* 关键的

key tree	密钥树
key component	关键组件
key element	关键要素
key point	关键点
key feature	关键特征

Two key concepts contribute to the creation of this environment.
两个关键概念打造了这一环境。

Day 52

linear

/ˈlɪniə(r)/ *adj.* 线性的

linear system	线性系统
linear combination	线性组合
linear regression	线性回归
linear approximation	线性近似
linear relationship	线性关系

From the linear relationships identified in the model, we can infer three interesting conclusions.
从模型的线性关系中,我们可以得出三个有趣结论。

interface

/ˈɪntəfeɪs/ *n.* 界面

user interface	用户界面
network interface	网络接口
subdomain interface	子域界面
system interface	系统接口
service interface	服务界面

The authors proposed a design method that can be applied to new generations of user interfaces.
几位作者提出了一个可以用于全新用户界面的设计方法。

Day 53

threshold
/ˈθreʃhəʊld/ n. 门槛

threshold value	阈值
similarity threshold	相似度阈值
memory threshold	内存阈值
bandwidth threshold	带宽阈值

The threshold value is adaptively adjusted.
我们对阈值进行了相应的调整。

category
/ˈkætəgəri/ n. 类别

| category theory | 范畴论 |

It is very difficult to express the results using only conventional terminology, so some category theory terminology is necessary.
我们很难用传统术语解释结果,因此有必要采用范畴论术语。

Day 54

iteration
/ˌɪtəˈreɪʃn/ n. 迭代

Jacobi iteration	雅可比迭代
interface iteration	界面迭代
optimization iteration	优化迭代
successive iteration	逐次迭代

In contrast, this work's modeling is based on Jacobi iteration and binary arithmetic.
相反,这一工作模型基于雅可比迭代和二进制运算。

length

/leŋkθ/ n. 长度;字符串长度;向量元素数

path length	路径长度
sequence length	序列长度
maximum length	最大长度
average length	平均长度

This means that even in small-world networks with many nodes, the shortest path length between two individual nodes is likely to be relatively small.
这意味着甚至是在充满诸多节点的小世界网络中,两个子节点之间的最短路径很可能相当小。

Day 55

aspect

/ˈæspekt/ n. 方面

aspect ratio	纵横比;屏幕宽高比

Based on the area and aspect ratio of connected components, isolated text characters are extracted using area-histogram analysis.
基于区域和连接成分的纵横比,我们借助面积直方图分析提取了孤立文本字符。

failure

/ˈfeɪljə(r)/ n. 失败;失效;故障

node failure	节点故障
network failure	网络故障
system failure	系统故障
service failure	服务失败
hardware failure	硬件故障

The proposed techniques are fairly resilient to message losses and node failures.
这一策略下,信息不易丢失,也不容易出现节点故障。

Day 56

execution
/ˌeksɪˈkjuːʃn/ *n.* 执行

speculative **execution**	推测执行
task **execution**	任务执行
program **execution**	程序执行
code **execution**	代码执行
parallel **execution**	并行执行

In the remainder of this section, we describe how we address each of these three requirements, as well as where to predict and how to automatically transform plans for speculative execution.
本章剩余部分,我们描述如何处理这三项要求、预测并为接下来的推测执行制订自动转换计划。

process
/ˈprəʊses/ *v.* 处理

process the task	处理任务
process the search	处理搜索
process the query	处理查询

The default value is one, meaning that only a single user can process the task.
缺省值为 1,这意味着只有 1 个用户可以处理这个任务。

Day 57

architecture
/ˈɑːkɪtektʃə(r)/ *n.* 结构

software **architecture**	软件结构
system **architecture**	体系结构
network **architecture**	网络构架

| deep **architecture** | 深层结构 |
| security **architecture** | 安全结构 |

Many definitions of software architecture exist; however, there is no universally accepted definition.
软件结构有许多定义,然而人们尚未达成一致。

theory

/ˈθɪəri/ *n.* 理论

grounded **theory**	扎根理论
game **theory**	博弈理论
graph **theory**	图论
prototype **theory**	原型理论
information **theory**	信息论

The data analysis technique I use in this paper is inspired by grounded theory, which is just one form of data analysis with its limitations and advantages.
本论文中的数据分析策略受扎根理论启发,该理论是数据分析方法之一,有其劣势和优势。

Day 58

mapping

/ˈmæpɪŋ/ *n.* 映射

homeomorphic **mapping**	同胚映射
gradient **mapping**	渐变映射
mapping function	映射函数
mapping system	映射系统

The observed data set X can be transformed into a higher dimensional feature space by applying a nonlinear mapping function to achieve nonlinear separation.
观察到的数据集 X 可以借助非线性映射函数实现非线性分离,转换为一个更高维的特征空间。

configuration

/kənˌfɪɡəˈreɪʃən/ n. 布局;构造;配置

model **configuration**	模型配置
initial **configuration**	初始配置
network **configuration**	网络配置
optimal **configuration**	优化配置
system **configuration**	系统配置

Industrial feature models may consist of hundreds of features which increases the complexity of feature model configuration.
工业特征模型可能包含上百个特征,这使得特征模型的配置较为复杂。

Day 59

phase

/feɪz/ n. 阶段

phase flow	相流动
phase transition	相变
phase space	相空间
phase diagram	相图

A phase diagram can be used to view the behavior of a total system and can be used to illustrate the how changed values impacts the whole system.
相图可以用来考察整个系统的行为,阐述发生变化的价值如何影响整个系统。

enable

/ɪˈneɪbl/ v. 启动

enable the partitioning	实现分割
enable the fetching of data	实现数据抓取
enable data to be transformed	实现数据转换
enable the user to find an item of interest	帮助用户找到感兴趣的项目

A high degree of monitoring will enable the flow of information.
较高检测水平将会实现信息流动。

Day 60

assign

/əˈsaɪn/ *v.* 分配；布置

assign the user to a server	将用户分配给一个服务器
assign the right number of resources	分配适量的资源
assign the same label	分配相同的标签
assign values	为……赋值

To assign the user to a server, the mapping system bases its answers on large amounts of historical and current data.
为了将用户分配给一个服务器，映射系统基于大量历史和现存数据给出答案。

organization

/ˌɔːɡənaɪˈzeɪʃn/ *n.* 组织

virtual organization	虚拟组织
project organization	项目组织
hierarchical organization	分层组织
development organization	发展组织

A virtual organization for clinicians and scientists who require access to grid resources can be created.
我们可以为需要网格资源的临床医生和科学家创建一个虚拟组织。

Day 61

metric

/ˈmetrɪk/ *n.* 度量

distance metric	距离度量
security metric	安全度量

| performance **metric** | 绩效指标 |
| evaluation **metric** | 评价指标 |

Today's security metrics are typically based on two assumptions.
当今的安全度量主要基于两个假设。

argument
/ˈɑːɡjumənt/ *n.* 论据,理由

| **argument** system | 论证系统 |
| **argument** framework | 论证框架 |

We make one further assumption regarding the structure of argument systems.
我们可以针对论证系统的结构提出另一个假设。

Day 62

combination
/ˌkɒmbɪˈneɪʃn/ *n.* 组合

combination coefficient	组合系数
combination method	组合方法
combination value	组合值

This study uses a combination method of normative analysis and empirical analysis.
本研究主要采用实证和规范组合的研究方法。

mesh
/meʃ/ *n.* 网格

wireless **mesh**	无线网状网
computational **mesh**	计算网格
mesh refinement	网格细化
mesh optimization	网格优化

The major advantages of wireless mesh networks are high data support.
无线网状网的主要优势是大量数据支持。

Day 63

spatial
/ˈspeɪʃl/ *adj.* 空间的

spatial resolution	空间分辨率
spatial distribution	空间分布
spatial information	空间信息
spatial variation	空间变异
spatial pattern	空间模式

To accomplish this aim, the spatial information is input to the network.
为完成这一目标,我们把空间信息输入了网络。

proof
/pruːf/ *n.* 证据

mathematical proof	数学证明
formal proof	形式证法;形式证明

Their analysis includes mathematical proofs on selecting such node sets.
他们的分析包括选择这些节点集的数学证明。

Day 64

assumption
/əˈsʌmpʃn/ *n.* 假设;假定

underlying assumption	潜在假设
reasonable assumption	合理假设
simplifying assumption	简化假设
unrealistic assumption	不现实的假设

There seems to be an underlying assumption that some things can be correctly predicted while others cannot.
似乎存在一个潜在假设,有些事物可以正确预测,而有些则不行。

cell

/sel/ *n.* 单元;电解槽;电池

grid **cell**	网格单元
cell phone	电话
cell value	单元值
cell model	电解槽模型

The cell phone shall go into a charge mode when the unit is plugged in.
当我们插入这一单元,手机就会进入充电模式。

Day 65

computation

/ˌkɒmpjuˈteɪʃn/ *n.* 计算;计算过程

computation time	计算时间
computation tree	计算树
computation path	计算路径
computation complexity	计算复杂度

Finally, we give an indication about the system's computation time.
最后,我们暗示了系统的计算时间。

approximation

/əˌprɒksɪˈmeɪʃn/ *n.* 粗略估计;近似值

approximation algorithm	近似算法
approximation scheme	近似方案
approximation error	近似误差

In the mentioned paper, a greedy approximation algorithm is proposed for solving the problem.
为了解决问题,本文提出了贪婪近似算法。

Day 66

operator
/ˈɒpəreɪtə(r)/ *n.* 操作员；运算符

multiplication **operator**	乘法算子
system **operator**	系统操作员
network **operator**	网络运营商
aggregation **operator**r	集成算子

We found that there was no effect of the aggregation operator on the predictions.
我们发现集成算子并不会对预测产生影响。

file
/faɪl/ *n.* 文件

file descriptor	文件描述符
file name	文件名
file recovery	文件恢复
file server	文件服务器

We use the list of file names and corresponding revision numbers to download the files.
我们采用了文件名列表和对应的修改数字来下载文件。

Day 67

kernel
/ˈkɜːnl/ *n.* 内核

polynomial **kernel**	多项式核
Gaussian **kernel**	高斯核
kernel function	核函数
kernel parameter	核心参数

We test and compare various kernel function performances by using different types of datasets.
我们用不同类型的数据集测试和比较核函数的表现。

store

/stɔː(r)/ *v.* 存储

store the results	存储结果
store the information	存储信息
store the data	存储数据
store the parameter	存储参数

Store the data into the database.
将数据存储到数据库中。

Day 68

subset

/ˈsʌbset/ *n.* 子集

feature **subset**	特征子集
optimal **subset**	最佳子集
maximal **subset**	最大子集
minimal **subset**	最小子集

We can remove a minimal subset.
我们可以去掉最小子集。

memory

/ˈmeməri/ *n.* 记忆；存储器

memory access	内存访问
memory requirements	内存需求
memory usage	内存使用
memory consumption	内存消耗

It currently gathers memory statistics via the interface.
它目前通过界面收集内存数据。

Day 69

capability

/ˌkeɪpəˈbɪləti/ *n.* 能力

capability maturity	能力成熟度
capability development	能力发展
capability assessment	能力评估
capability level	能力等级

This model supports not only software development but also software capability assessment.
这一模型不仅支持软件开发,也支持软件能力评估。

cluster

/ˈklʌstə(r)/ *v.* 群聚;聚集;聚类

cluster the sample of 15 datasets	实现 15 个数据集样本聚类
cluster the location	实现地点聚类
cluster the sequence	序列聚类

Table 2 summarizes the amount of time required by each algorithm we tested to cluster the sample of 15 datasets.
表 2 总结了每种算法需要的时间,实现 15 个数据集样本聚类。

Day 70

variation

/ˌveəriˈeɪʃn/ *n.* 变异;变化

variation point	变异位点
variation realization	变异实现
variation range	变化范围
variation method	变分法;差异法

For simplicity in our example, we have only used two variation realization relations.
为了在例子中简化,我们只使用了两种变异实现关系。

similarity

/ˌsɪməˈlærəti/ *n.* 相似点；近似点

similarity measure	相似性测度；相似性度量
similarity value	相似度值
similarity threshold	相似度阈值
similarity matrix	相似度矩阵

The cosine similarity measure we use calculates the angle between normalised hybrid vectors.
我们采用的余弦相似度测量值计算了标准混合向量的角度。

Day 71

bug

/bʌg/ *n.* 漏洞

bug fixing	漏洞修复
bug report	漏洞报告
bug prediction	漏洞预测
bug tracking	错误追踪
bug summary	错误总结

For any given bug report, first we identified the high-level reason and checked if the reason already fits into any of the existing categories.
对于每一项漏洞报告，我们首先找出了深层次原因，然后检查现有原因是否属于已有类别。

choice

/tʃɔɪs/ *n.* 选择

optimal choice	最佳选择
particular choice	特定选择
appropriate choice	合适的选择
arbitrary choice	任意选择

The best choice of memory length also differs in value before and after the change.
在改变之后,记忆长度的最佳选择值也有所不同。

Day 72

dimension

/daɪˈmenʃn/ *n.* 维度

temporal **dimension**	时间维度
spatial **dimension**	空间维度
additional **dimension**	额外维度
local **dimension**	局部维度,局部维数

For each spatial dimension, we apply numerical schemes.
对于每一个空间维度,我们都采用了数值化方案。

uncertainty

/ʌnˈsɜːtnti/ *n.* 不确定性;平均信息量

model **uncertainty**	模型不确定性
epistemic **uncertainty**	认知不确定性
cumulative **uncertainty**	累积不确定性
measurement **uncertainty**	测量不确定性

For a given set of inputs, model uncertainty is smaller over larger catchment areas.
对于既定输入,对于更大的集水区,模型不确定性更小。

Day 73

numerical

/njuːˈmerɪkl/ *adj.* 数字的;数值的

numerical experiment	数值实验
numerical solution	数值解决方案

numerical vector	数值向量
numerical integration	数值积分
numerical simulation	数值模拟

The numerical experiments were executed for the problem shown in Fig. 3.
对于图 3 中的问题，我们采用了数值实验。

request

/rɪˈkwest/ n. 请求

authentication request	身份验证请求
reservation request	预定请求
examination request	监测要求
end-to-end request	端对端请求

Thus, an optimal scenario would have been to reject the end-to-end request and allow the acceptance of the shorter requests.
因此，最优解决方案是拒绝端对端请求，允许接收更短的请求。

Day 74

extract

/ˈekstrækt/ v. 选取；提取

extract the data	提取数据
extract the structure	提取结构
extract the watermark	提取水印

This cross-check helped the team to extract the data and conduct the measurement in a reliable manner.
这种交叉验证帮助团队提取数据，并以可靠的方式进行验证。

layer

/ˈleɪə(r)/ n. 层

hidden layer	隐藏层
application layer	应用层

network **layer**	网络层
output **layer**	输出层

What metadata do we preserve at the network layer?
我们在网络层保留怎样的元数据？

Day 75

extension

/ɪkˈstenʃn/ *n.* 扩充；扩展

security **extension**	安全扩展；安全性延伸
semantic **extension**	语义扩展
probabilistic **extension**	概率性扩展

We argue that it may be time to develop a security extension for the USB protocol.
我们认为现在正是为 USB 协议打造安全扩展的时候。

machine

/məˈʃiːn/ *n.* 机器

machine learning	机器学习
machine translation	机器翻译
machine precision	机器精度
machine running	机器运行

Both of these problems can potentially be addressed via machine learning techniques.
这两个问题都可能借助机器学习解决。

Day 76

characteristic

/ˌkærəktəˈrɪstɪk/ *n.* 特征；特点；特色

characteristic function	特征函数
characteristic polynomial	特征多项式

| characteristic length | 特征长度 |
| characteristic point | 特征点 |

The representation of the characteristic function may be exponential in the number of tasks.
特征函数在任务中的表现可能是呈指数增长的。

computer

/kəmˈpjuːtə(r)/ *n.* 计算机

computer security	计算机安全
computer science	计算机科学
computer network	计算机网络
computer system	计算机系统

Network and computer attacks have become pervasive in today's world.
网络和计算机攻击在当今世界十分普遍。

Day 77

finite

/ˈfaɪnaɪt/ *adj.* 有限的；限定的

finite element	有限元素
finite number	有限数
finite volume	有限体积
finite time	有限时间

This is modeled using finite element method.
这是用有限元素方法进行模拟的。

dynamic

/daɪˈnæmɪk/ *adj.* 充满活力的；动态的

dynamic programming	动态规划
dynamic trigger	动态触发器
dynamic capabilities	动态能力
dynamic nature	动态特性

We developed a computer program, to implement the dynamic programming algorithm.
我们设计了一个计算机程序来实现动态规划算法。

Day 78

profile
/ˈprəʊfaɪl/ n. 配置文件

personality **profile**	个性特征描述
user **profile**	用户配置文件
load **profile**	负荷特征
concentration **profile**	浓度剖面
surface **profile**	表面轮廓

Our ANOVA test result indeed confirmed that the range of personality profiles among these members was significantly different.
我们的方差分析测试结果的确证实不同用户的个性特征存在显著差异。

classifier
/ˈklæsɪfaɪə(r)/ n. 分类器

SVM **classifier**	支持向量机分类器
pattern **classifier**	模式分类器
binary **classifier**	二元分类器
Bayesian **classifier**	贝叶斯分类器

This approach provides us with an efficient way for describing arbitrary binary classifiers.
这一方法为我们提供了描述任意二元分类器的有效方式。

Day 79

analyze
/ˈænəlaɪz/ v. 对……分析;分解

analyze the effect	分析影响
analyze the performance	分析表现
analyze the security	分析安全性
analyze the result	分析结果

By reason of the previous statement, it is important to analyze the effect in a situation in which the available network bandwidth decreases.
根据先前的声明,重要的是在现有网络带宽降低的情况下分析影响。

coefficient
/ˌkəʊɪˈfɪʃnt/ n. 系数

correlation coefficient	相关系数
wavelet coefficient	小波系数
runoff coefficient	径流系数
expansion coefficient	膨胀系数
input coefficient	输入系数

The Spearman's rank correlation coefficient (rs) is a number ranging from -1 to $+1$.
斯皮尔曼等级相关系数的数值在-1和$+1$之间。

Day 80

form
/fɔːm/ v. (使)出现;(使)形成

form the basis	成为……的基础
form the core	成为……的核心

In this section we present the games that form the basis of our empirical analysis.
本节中我们展示了构成实证分析游戏的基础。

developer
/dɪˈveləpə(r)/ n. 开发商

core developer	核心开发人员
software developer	软件开发商

application **developer**	应用程序开发员
system **developer**	系统开发人员

We propose requirements for a tool to support personnel from Chief Security Officers (CSOs) and business managers to software developers and system administrators.
我们为一个工具提出需求,支持各类人员,包括首席安全官、业务经理、软件开发商和系统管理员。

Day 81

reference

/ˈrefrəns/ *n.* 基准

reference monitor	基准监视器
reference set	参考集
reference relation	引用关系
reference frame	参考系

Both platforms implement a reference monitor.
两个平台都设置了一个基准监视器。

attribute

/əˈtrɪbjuːt/ *n.* 特征;属性

quality **attribute**	质量属性
security **attribute**	安全属性
theoretical **attribute**	理论属性
physical **attribute**	物理属性

We evaluate the environment using so called quality attributes as introduced in Section 3.
我们用第三节中介绍的质量属性评估环境。

Day 82

correlation

/ˌkɒrəˈleɪʃn/ *n.* 相互关系;关联

positive **correlation**	正相关
negative **correlation**	负相关
rank **correlation**	秩相关
Pearson **correlation**	皮尔逊相关
Spearman **correlation**	斯皮尔曼相关

There will be a positive correlation between social interaction (quality and quantity) and transactive memory.
社交互动（质量和数量）和交互记忆之间存在正相关关系。

map

/mæp/ *n.* 映射；存储转换；地图

depth **map**	深度图
salience **map**	显著性地图
topological **map**	拓扑地图
disparity **map**	视差图

We can then improve the accuracy of the illumination conditions, which in turn improves the depth map.
我们可以改善照明条件的准确度，反过来改善深度图。

Day 83

vulnerability (vulnerabilities)

/ˌvʌlnərəˈbɪləti/(/ˌvʌlnərəˈbɪlətiz/) *n.* 漏洞

security **vulnerabilities**	安全漏洞
legal **vulnerabilities**	法律漏洞
potential **vulnerabilities**	潜在漏洞
software **vulnerabilities**	软件漏洞
system **vulnerabilities**	系统漏洞

Several vulnerabilities have been found in Java verifiers.
我们已经在Java验证器中发现了许多系统漏洞。

physical

/ˈfɪzɪkl/ *adj.* 物理的

physical process	物理过程
physical machine	物理机
physical server	物理服务器
physical location	实际位置

These models attempt to describe the physical processes that control energy and mass transfers in the soil.
这些模型尝试描述控制土壤中能量和质量传递的物理过程。

Day 84

Internet

/ˈɪntənet/ *n.* 网络

Internet Explorer	IE 浏览器
Internet service	网络服务
Internet traffic	互联网流量
Internet access	互联网接入

The introduction of Internet access to the R&D department of a manufacturing organisation would permit rapid and extensive competitor analysis.
将互联网引入制造机构的研发部门将带来迅速、广泛的竞争分析。

prediction

/prɪˈdɪkʃn/ *n.* 预言之事；预测（行为）

prediction model	预测模型
prediction system	预测系统
prediction framework	预测框架

The plots show that the prediction models.
这些图片展示了预测模型。

Day 85

processing
/ˈprəʊsesɪŋ/ n. 加工；处理；运算

information processing	信息处理
language processing	语言处理
image processing	图像处理
query processing	询问处理

The understanding of information processing in biological and social networks has inspired novel AI techniques.
对生物和社会网络信息处理的理解启发了全新 AI 技术。

optimization
/ˌɒptɪmaɪˈzeɪʃn/ n. 最优化；最佳化

global optimization	全局优化
black-box optimization	黑盒优化
stochastic optimization	随机优化
parameter optimization	参数优化

This study considers the following global optimization problems.
本研究考虑到了如下全球优化问题。

Day 86

specification
/ˌspesɪfɪˈkeɪʃn/ n. 规格；规范；说明书

formal specification	形式规范
requirements specification	需求规格说明书
functional specification	功能规格说明
system specification	系统规格

Formal methods is the mathematical specification, design and verification of computer systems.
形式方法是数学规范、设计和验证计算机系统的方法。

equal

/ˈiːkwəl/ *adj.* 平等的

equal number	相等数字
equal probability	等概率
equal weight	等权重
equal importance	同样重要

All violations are serious and are of equal importance.
所有违反规则的情况都很严重和同等重要。

Day 87

frequency

/ˈfriːkwənsi/ *n.* 频率

high **frequency**	高频率
low **frequency**	低频率
minimum **frequency**	最低频率
maximum **frequency**	最高频率

It is reported that utterances with happiness emotion have high energy at high frequency range.
据说,表达快乐情绪的话语在高频区间能量值更高。

cyber

/saɪbə(r)/ *adj.* 网络的

cyber crime	网络犯罪
cyber warfare	网络战
cyber security	网络安全
cyber weapon	网络武器
cyber attack	网络袭击

Technological advance may immediately reduce cyber crime incidents; however, criminals will soon catch up by exploiting loopholes in the new systems.
技术进步可能会迅速减少网络犯罪事件。然而，罪犯可能将很快抓住并利用新系统中的漏洞。

Day 88

basic

/ˈbeɪsɪk/ *adj.* 最重要的；基本的

basic idea	基本概念
basic block	基本块
basic feature	基本特征
basic method	基本方法

Our basic idea is to employ planning techniques for solving the configuration problem.
我们最基本的概念是采用规划策略解决配置问题。

testing

/ˈtestɪŋ/ *n.* 试验；测验

penetration testing	渗透测试
hypothesis testing	假设检验
application testing	应用试验
statistical testing	统计检验
software testing	软件测试

As it has been discussed and defined in software testing books, testing level in this context denotes, in an abstract viewpoint, the granularity of testing.
正如软件测试书籍中讨论和定义的那样，从抽象角度看，测试水平暗示了测试颗粒度。

Day 89

engineering

/ˌendʒɪˈnɪərɪŋ/ *n.* 工程

software **engineering**	软件工程
reverse **engineering**	逆向工程
ontology **engineering**	本体工程
feature **engineering**	特征工程
traffic **engineering**	交通工程

Our aim in this paper is to present a collection of conceptual, security engineering tools supporting the design and analysis of distributed authorization infrastructures.
本文的研究目的是展示一系列有关概念和安全工程工具,支持分布式授权基础设施的设计和分析。

experimental

/ɪkˌsperɪˈmentl/ *adj.* 试验的

experimental evaluation	试验评价
experimental data	试验数据
experimental setup	试验设置
experimental results	试验结果
experimental study	试验研究

The validity of results of an experimental evaluation is always subject to different threats including internal and external threats.
试验评价的有效性常常受到内部和外部威胁影响。

Day 90

write

/raɪt/ *v.* 写入

write the solution	写入解决方案
write the rules	写入规则
write the information	写入信息
write the data	写入数据

We write the solution in the form.
我们在表格中写入了解决方案。

efficiency

/ɪˈfɪʃnsi/ n. 效率

computational **efficiency**	计算效率
energy **efficiency**	能源效率
model **efficiency**	模型效率
space **efficiency**	空间效率
search **efficiency**	搜索效率

To alleviate this problem new computational technologies are making the goal of sufficient computational efficiency more and more realizable.
为了缓和这一问题，新的计算技术使得我们达成计算效率目标变得越来越可靠。

Day 91

correspond

/ˌkɒrəˈspɒnd/ v. 相一致；符合

correspond with the claims	和……的声明保持一致
correspond with the changes	与……的变化一致
correspond with our overall metrics	与我们的总体数据相对应

The first three hypotheses correspond with the attitudinal variables.
起初三个假设与态度变量相对应。

statistical

/stəˈtɪstɪkl/ adj. 数据的；统计的

statistical analysis	数据分析
statistical significance	统计显著性
statistical model	统计模型
statistical testing	统计测试
statistical measures	统计措施

The sample sizes were too small to allow for strong statistical analysis beyond descriptive statistics.
样本数据太小，除了描述性统计外不适合较强统计分析。

Day 92

return

/rɪˈtɜːn/ *v.* 返回;回车

return the same result	返回相同结果
return the answer	返回答案
return the value	返回值

They may sometimes return the answer "unknown" in response to queries.
对于一些检索,它们有时会返回"未知"的答案。

base

/beɪs/ *n.* 根基;根部

base data	基础数据
base system	基础系统
base node	根节点,基本节点
base server	基础服务器
information **base**	信息库

The described methodology was applied on a real data base.
描述的方法应用于真实基础数据。

Day 93

address

/əˈdres/ *n.* 网址;地址

Email **address**	电子邮件地址
destination **address**	目的地地址
network **address**	网络地址
physical **address**	物理地址
memory **address**	内存地址

We use the physical address converted from the virtual address to avoid ambiguity.
我们采用了从虚拟地址转化的物理地址来避免模糊。

link

/lɪŋk/ v. 连接

link the position	把两个位置连接在一起
link the information	把信息连接在一起
link the elements	把元素连接在一起

The arrows link these elements with corresponding representation in the model.
箭头将这些要素与模型中相应表示链接起来。

Day 94

velocity

/vəˈlɒsəti/ n. 速度，速率

velocity field	速度场
velocity profile	速度剖面
velocity vector	速度矢量
velocity distribution	速度分布
velocity component	速度分量，分速度

Also, v denotes the velocity vector of the adjacent element.
同时，v 表示临近元素的速度向量。

sensor

/ˈsensə(r)/ n. 传感器；敏感元件；探测设备

sensor data	传感器数据
sensor network	传感器网络
sensor node	传感器节点
sensor system	传感器系统
sensor time	传感器时间

In a typical scenario, temperature values are collected from the sensor network.
在特定的情况下，气温值通过传感器网络收集。

Day 95

share

/ʃeə(r)/ v. 分享

share the principle	共享一个原则
share the premise	共享一个前提
share the location	共享一个位置

Both share the principle of communication interfaces.
两者共享通信接口原则。

theorem

/ˈθɪərəm/ n. 定理

representation theorem	表示定理
Bayes theorem	贝叶斯定理
interpolation theorem	内插定理,插值定理
divergence theorem	散度定理

To overcome this problem, we use Bayes theorem.
为解决这一问题,我们采用了贝叶斯定理。

Day 96

execute

/ˈeksɪkjuːt/ v. 执行;运行

execute phase	执行阶段
execute step	执行步骤
execute state	执行状态

Both share the principle of communication interfaces.
两者共享通信接口原则。

core

/kɔː(r)/ *n.* 内核

core vector	核心向量
core asset	核心财富,核心资产
core computing	核心计算
core business	核心业务

We used core developers as our units of analysis and made comparisons across project phases.
我们将核心开发人员作为分析单元,并对不同的项目阶段进行比较。

Day 97

update

/ˌʌpˈdeɪt/ *v.* 更新;为……增加信息

update the value	更新值
update the statistical parameter	更新统计参数
update the vector	更新向量

To estimate and update the statistical parameters more accurately, another algorithm is proposed.
为了更准确地预估和更新统计参数,我们提出了另一个算法。

constant

/ˈkɒnstənt/ *adj.* 恒定的,不变的

constant value	常数值
constant time	常数时间
constant factor	常数因子
constant velocity	恒定速度

This constant value should be low enough to observe the network behavior for the high-speed network.
为了观察高速网络的表现,常数值应当足够低。

Day 98

hypothesis

/haɪˈpɒθəsɪs/ *n.* 假设

null **hypothesis**	零假设
induction **hypothesis**	归纳假设
statistical **hypothesis**	统计假设
inductive **hypothesis**	归纳假设

We use a statistical test to determine whether we should accept or reject the null hypothesis.
我们采用统计检验来决定是否应该接受或拒绝零假设。

label

/ˈleɪbl/ *n.* 标签;标记

label switching	标签交换
label image	标签图像
label similarity	标签相似性
label information	标签信息

We again add the previous iteration of the label function to the graph.
我们再次把先前标签功能迭代添加到了图表上。

Day 99

capacity

/kəˈpæsəti/ *n.* 能力;容积

capacity efficiency	能力效率
capacity constraint	产能限制
capacity planning	产能规划
capacity network	网络能力

Overall the capacity efficiency of the hierarchical protection tree was between 20% and 27%

less than the optimal tree design.
总体来说，分层保护树的产能效率比最优树形设计低 20%～27%。

infrastructure

/ˈɪnfrəstrʌktʃə(r)/ *n.* 基础设施

infrastructure architecture	基础设施构架
infrastructure factor	基础设施因素
infrastructure provider	基础设施提供商
infrastructure protection	基础设施保护

Here, a 3-tier layered infrastructure architecture pattern is used for the order processing, product management and financial applications.
此处一个三层基础设施构架模式用于订单处理、产品管理和财务应用。

Day 100

expression

/ɪkˈspreʃn/ *n.* 表达式；表达

expression recognition	表情识别
expression data	表达数据
expression statement	表达式语句
expression mechanism	表达机制

We propose a feasible algorithm for manifold facial expression recognition.
我们提出了一个可行算法，用于实现多重面部表情识别。

noise

/nɔɪz/ *n.* 噪声

noise removal	去噪
noise density	噪声密度
noise component	噪声分量
noise robustness	噪声鲁棒性

In this paper, we restrict our attention to a mixed noise removal task.
本文中，我们将注意力集中于一项混合降噪任务。

第二部分
四星词汇

Day 101

pixel
/ˈpɪksl/ n. 像素

pixel value	像素值
pixel accuracy	像素精度
pixel intensity	像素强度
pixel matching	像素配准

A common method used to model the distribution of individual pixel values makes use of probability density functions.
模拟个体像素值分布的一个常见方法是概率密度函数。

client
/ˈklaɪənt/ n. 客户

client application	客户应用程序
client project	客户端项目
client code	客户端代码
client host	表达机制

A client application can thus perform any action against this resource.
因此,客户应用程序可以针对这种资源实施任何行动。

Day 102

formula
/ˈfɔːmjələ/ n. 公式;方程式;方案

propositional **formula**	命题公式
probability **formula**	概率公式
interpolation **formula**	插值公式
chemical **formula**	化学公式

Every propositional formula can be reduced to conjunctive normal form.
每一个命题公式都可以简化为合取范式。

interval

/ˈɪntəvl/ n. 间隙；间隔

interval number	区间数
interval level	区间等级
interval framework	区间框架

The average recognition rate, standard deviation and 95% confidence interval level for all the above algorithms were computed.
上述所有算法的平均识别速度、标准差和95%的置信水平都被计算了出来。

Day 103

storage

/ˈstɔːrɪdʒ/ n. 存储

data storage	数据存储
cloud storage	云存储
temporary storage	临时存储
maximum storage	最大存储

A significant challenge associated with this distributed data storage approach is that resources and expertise are required to implement the tools at each local research site.
分布式数据存储中一个重大挑战是我们需要资源和技术来补充每一个本地研究网站所需的工具。

classify

/ˈklæsɪfaɪ/ v. 把……分类；把……分级

classify the model	对模型进行分类
classify the property	对性质进行分类
classify the shape	对形状进行分类

We think that this methodology makes it easier and more objective to classify the models according to their performance.
我们认为采用这种方法根据模型表现分类更容易，也更客观。

Day 104

topology
/təˈpɒlədʒi/ *n.* 拓扑学

network **topology**	网络拓扑结构
overlay **topology**	覆盖拓扑,覆盖网拓扑
physical **topology**	物理拓扑,实体布局
geometry **topology**	几何拓扑

Interestingly, among the existing Internet topology generators, none has yet been widely accepted as sufficiently accurate.
有趣的是,现有网络拓扑生成器中,人们普遍认为没有一个是完全准确的。

consistent
/kənˈsɪstənt/ *adj.* 一致的;连贯的

consistent result	一致的结果
consistent solution	一致的解决方案
consistent network	一致的网络
consistent formula	一致的公式

We are only likely to find reliable and consistent results when the experiment is done carefully.
只有我们仔细进行实验,才能得到可靠、一致的结果。

Day 105

transformation
/ˌtrænsfəˈmeɪʃn/ *n.* 改变;转变

data **transformation**	数据转换
syntactic **transformation**	语法转换,句法转换
linear **transformation**	线性变换
parameter **transformation**	参数变换

This is in contrast to the regression operator, which is a purely syntactic transformation.
这与回归运算相反,完全是一种句法转换。

density

/ˈdensəti/ *n.* 密度

probability **density**	概率密度
electronic **density**	电子密度
network **density**	线网密度,网络密度
bulk **density**	体积密度

Three different terrain types (i. e., urban, suburban and rural) are defined to investigate the impact of network population density.
我们定义了三种地形(城市、郊区和乡村)来调查网络人口密度的影响。

Day 106

estimation

/ˌestɪˈmeɪʃn/ *n.* 估计;估算;评价

estimation method	估计方法
estimation technique	估算技术
estimation process	评估过程
estimation framework	估算框架

If project managers were better educated in estimation techniques and methodologies, they could improve their effort.
如果项目经理在估算技术和方法上得到了更好的培训,他们就可以更加努力。

map

/mæp/ *v.* 绘制……的地图;映射

map the point	绘制点
map the data	绘制数据
map the structure	绘制结构

The first step required is to define an ontology on which to map the data provided by the Web Service.
所需第一步是定义本体,描绘网络服务提供的数据。

Day 107

validation
/ˌvælɪˈdeɪʃn/ *n.* 验证；确认

cross **validation**	交叉验证
empirical **validation**	实证验证
experimental **validation**	实验验证
input **validation**	输入验证

Through a cross validation evaluation, we showed that only a small number of instances of each type are required for simple appliances.
通过交叉验证评价，我们发现对于简单电器来说，每类需要的实例较少。

ratio
/ˈreɪʃiəʊ/ *n.* 比例；比率

likelihood **ratio**	似然比
compression **ratio**	压缩比
detection **ratio**	探测比
competitive **ratio**	竞争比

In order to compare our illumination correction method, we have used the PCA-LDA likelihood ratio classifier.
为了比较我们的照明校正法，我们已经采用了主成分提取——线性判别分析似然比分类器。

Day 108

minimum
/ˈmɪnɪməm/ *adj.* 最小的；最低限度的

minimum number	最小数字
minimum value	最小值
minimum distance	最小距离
minimum sensitivity	最低灵敏度

The mean accuracy and minimum sensitivity and the mean ranking are also included in Table 4.
平均准确度、最低灵敏度和平均排名同样包含在表 4 中。

bandwidth

/ˈbændwɪdθ/ *n.* 带宽

network **bandwidth**	网络带宽
optimal **bandwidth**	最优带宽
total **bandwidth**	总带宽
maximum **bandwidth**	最大带宽

Three black-box profiles are maintained per virtual server: CPU utilization, network bandwidth utilization and swap rate.
每个虚拟服务器中保留了三项黑盒配置文件:CPU 利用率、网络带宽和互换利率。

Day 109

concentration

/ˌkɒnsnˈtreɪʃn/ *n.* 集中;浓度

vapor **concentration**	水汽浓度
pollutant **concentration**	污染物浓度
nutrient **concentration**	营养浓度
pesticide **concentration**	农药浓度
background **concentration**	背景浓度

Fig. 2 shows the cross section of the contaminant concentration distribution obtained using the typical 3D numerical model.
图 2 展示了通过典型 3D 数字模型获取的污染浓度分布的横截面。

underlie

/ˌʌndəˈlaɪ/ *v.* 构成……的基础

| **underlie** the software | 构成软件的基础 |
| **underlie** the results | 构成结果的基础 |

The correctness of the scientific and mathematical models that underlie the software is a key factor in the accuracy of results.
科学和数学模型正确与否是构成软件准确度的重要因素。

Day 110

calculation
/ˌkælkjuˈleɪʃn/ *n.* 计算,运算;估算

force **calculation**	力的计算
risk **calculation**	危险计算
distance **calculation**	距离计算
similarity **calculation**	相似度计算

To obtain faster convergence, force calculation order of nodes is randomly determined.
为了更快实现聚合,我们随机确认了节点力度计算顺序。

formulation
/ˌfɔːmjuˈleɪʃn/ *n.* 构想;阐述方法;公式化

mathematical **formulation**	数学公式
query **formulation**	查询公式
variational **formulation**	变分公式化

Further details on the model and on the mathematical formulation of each process are provided in the Appendix.
模型更多细节和每一步骤的数学公式详见附录。

Day 111

curve
/kɜːv/ *n.* 曲线;弧线

learning **curve**	学习曲线
evolving **curve**	演化曲线
progress **curve**	发展曲线

Further details on the model and on the mathematical formulation of each process are provided in the Appendix.
模型更多细节和每一步骤的数学公式详见附录。

chain

/tʃeɪn/ *n.* 单链表;有向链表

chain model	链模型
chain management	链管理
chain matrices	链矩阵

We aim to analyze the abstract Markov chain model.
我们的目的是研究抽象马尔可夫链模型。

Day 112

block

/blɒk/ *n.* 字块;分程序;块

block cipher	分组密码
block code	信息组代码
block length	封闭区段长度;字块长度
block retrieval	分块检索

The calculation of these transition probabilities follows the principle of sliding block code.
这些转移概率的计算遵循滑动信息组代码的原则。

online

/ˌɒnˈlaɪn/ *adj.* 线上的

online algorithm	线上算法
online service	线上服务
online data	线上数据
online repository	线上存储
online search	线上搜索

We devise a randomized online algorithm.
我们设计了一个随机线上算法。

Day 113

signature
/ˈsɪgnətʃə(r)/ *n.* 签名,署名;特征;信号差

signature processing	信号处理
signature verification	签名验证
signature file	签名文件
signature analysis	符号差分析

Each layer includes independently tunable monitors that combine signature analysis with statistical profiling.
每一层都包含独立可调谐的监视器,将符号差和统计分析结合在了一起。

partition
/pɑːˈtɪʃn/ *n.* 分区

partition problem	分区问题
partition boundary	分区边界
service **partition**	服务分区

The partition problem is solved.
分区问题得到了解决。

Day 114

vertex
/ˈvɜːteks/ *n.* 顶点;头顶

vertex set	顶点集
vertex degree	顶点度
vertex cover	点覆盖,顶点覆盖

The vertex set and edge set of the line graph are defined as follows.
我们将折线图的顶点集和边集定义如下。

module

/ˈmɒdjuːl/ *n.* 模块

detection **module**	检测模块
control **module**	控制模块
management **module**	管理模组

Without error detection modules, soft errors during program execution are hard to be noticed.
如果没有错误检测模块,那么项目执行过程中的软错误很难被注意到。

Day 115

active

/ˈæktɪv/ *adj.* 活动的

active memory	快速存储器;主动式存储器;有源存储器
active filter	有源滤波器
active contour	有效轮廓

In the previous section we defined two types of active paths: simple active paths and compound active paths.
前一节我们定义了两种活动路径:简单活动路径和复合活动路径。

setting

/ˈsetɪŋ/ *n.* 设置

parameter **setting**	参数设置
experimental **setting**	实验装置
bandwidth **setting**	带宽设置
uniform **setting**	统一设置
default **setting**	默认设置

Many users will be relying entirely upon the suitability of the default settings.
许多用户将完全依赖默认设置的适用性。

Day 116

check

/tʃek/ *v.* 核查；核对

check the consistency	核查一致性
check the validity	核查有效性
check the model	核查模型
check the accuracy	核查准确度

It is therefore important to check the consistency of our findings as more 2011 and 2012 patent applications are made public.
随着更多 2011 和 2012 年的专利应用公开，核查研究结果的一致性至关重要。

key

/kiː/ *n.* 主键；密钥；关键字；操作键

public **key**	公钥
private **key**	私钥
secret **key**	密钥
dynamic **key**	动态密钥

Each person's public key is published, while the private key is kept secret.
每个人的公钥是公开的，而私钥是隐蔽的。

Day 117

volume

/ˈvɒljuːm/ *n.* 卷

volume method	容积法
volume balance	体积均衡
volume density	体积密度

A finite volume method is used for discretization of the governing equation.

我们采用了有限容积法来实现控制方程的离散化。

interpretation

/ɪnˌtɜːprəˈteɪʃn/ *n.* 解释

interpretation structure	解释结构
interpretation process	解释过程
physical **interpretation**	物理解释
data **interpretation**	数据解释

Data analysis and data interpretation that takes diverse perspectives into account is essential.
多角度数据分析和解读至关重要。

Day 118

encode

/ɪnˈkəʊd/ *v.* 把……译成密码；给……编码

encode the watchlist	对监视列表进行编码
encode the test	对测试进行编码
encode the system	对系统进行编码
encode the syntax	对语法进行编码

Bloom filters are employed to encode the watchlist to preserve the privacy of participants.
我们采用布隆过滤器对监视列表进行编码，保护参与者的隐私。

dynamics

/daɪˈnæmɪks/ *n.* 动力学；力学；力度变化

dislocation **dynamics**	错位动力学
system **dynamics**	系统动力学
fluid **dynamics**	流体动力学
vegetation **dynamics**	植被带动力学

The main purpose of this paper is to propose a simple interpolation method of finding Computational Fluid Dynamics (CFD) solution.
本文的主要研究目的是找到简单插值方法，找出计算流体动力学的解决方案。

Day 119

heuristic
/hjʊəˈrɪstɪk/ *adj.* 启发性的；探试的

heuristic function	启发式函数
heuristic teaching	启发式教学
heuristic algorithm	启发式算法
heuristic search	启发式搜索
heuristic feature	启发式特征

The author presented a heuristic algorithm based on shortest Spanning Tree (ST).
作者基于最短生成树给出了启发式算法。

stream
/striːm/ *n.* 数据流

stream function	流函数
stream control	流控制
stream boundary	流边界
stream processing	流水式处理

We recall that (in two dimensions) the velocity components are simply derivatives of the stream function.
我们回忆(在两个维度上)，速度分量仅仅是流函数的衍生物。

Day 120

channel
/ˈtʃænl/ *n.* 通道；信道；链接通道

channel routing	通道布线
channel level	通道水平
channel quality	通道质量
channel reservation	信道预留；信道预定

Channel routing considers connecting pins in the small gaps or channels between the cells of a chip.
通道布线指的是将芯片单元之间小间隙或者通道的个人识别号连接起来。

programming

/ˈprəʊɡræmɪŋ/ *n.* 设计；规划；编制程序

dynamic **programming**	动态规划
pair **programming**	结对编程
linear **programming**	线性规划
logic **programming**	逻辑编程
constraint **programming**	约束规划

For the transferable utility case, we make use of linear programming.
对于可转移效用的案例，我们可以采用线性规划。

Day 121

cycle

/ˈsaɪkl/ *n.* 周期；循环；回路

cycle assessment	循环评价
cycle length	周期长度
cycle time	周期时间
cycle simulation	周期模拟
cycle inventory	周期库存

Life Cycle Assessment (LCA) is a useful tool for systematically estimating the environmental impacts.
生命周期评估是系统预估环境影响的有效工具。

reasoning

/ˈriːzənɪŋ/ *n.* 推理；推论

automated **reasoning**	自动推理
practical **reasoning**	实际推理
logical **reasoning**	逻辑推理

common sense **reasoning**	常识推理
qualitative **reasoning**	定性推理

This precludes the use of regression for automated reasoning.
这阻止我们使用回归进行自动推理。

Day 122

planning

/ˈplænɪŋ/ *n.* 规划

path **planning**	路径规划
project **planning**	项目规划
temporal **planning**	时间规划
resource **planning**	资源规划

This is similar to the sorts of challenges faced in optimal robot path planning.
这与机器人最优路径规划中面临的各类挑战十分相似。

bound

/baʊnd/ *n.* 界

lower **bound**	下界
upper **bound**	上界
bound variable	约束变量

A bound interval consists of both a lower bound and an upper bound.
有界区间同时包括上界和下界。

Day 123

frame

/freɪm/ *n.* 帧；信息框；框架

frame relay	帧中继
frame boundary	帧边界
frame computer	框架计算机
frame exchange	帧交换

Almost all personal computers, mainframe computers, minicomputers, and all other digital devices of the sorts in use today, use general purpose operating systems.
几乎所有的个人计算机、大型计算机、迷你计算机和我们如今使用的各种数字设备,都使用了通用目的操作系统。

refinement

/rɪˈfaɪnmənt/ n. 精炼;精进;改善;优化

local refinement	局部细化
structural refinement	结构优化
hierarchical refinement	分层细化
goal refinement	目标求精

This means that the cost of data remapping can potentially be much less than in hierarchical refinement methods.
这意味着对数据进行重新映射的成本可能远低于分层细化的方法。

Day 124

functionality

/ˌfʌŋkʃəˈnæləti/ n. 功能;泛函性,函数性

core functionality	核心功能
security functionality	安全功能
software functionality	软件功能度
functionality limitation	功能限制
functionality verification	功能验证

Overlay networks have recently gained attention as a viable alternative to overcome functionality limitations of the Internet.
作为一种克服网络功能限制的可行替代方案,覆盖网络最近吸引了人们的注意力。

logic

/ˈlɒdʒɪk/ *n.* 逻辑；推理方法

logic programming	逻辑编程
logic knowledge	逻辑知识
logic connection	逻辑连接
logic language	逻辑语言

Other approaches are based on description logics, such as inductive logic programming.
其余方法基于描述逻辑，例如归纳逻辑编程。

Day 125

empirical

/ɪmˈpɪrɪkl/ *adj.* 实证的

empirical study	实证研究
empirical evidence	实证证据
empirical software	实证软件
empirical evaluation	实证评价

This paper includes empirical evidence that companies must look at security laws, in addition to standards, to ensure reasonable security in information technology.
本研究采用实证证据说明，想要确保信息技术的相对安全，公司除了关注标准，还需要关注安全法律。

label

/ˈleɪbl/ *v.* 为……贴标签

label the topic	为话题打标签
label the stage	为不同阶段打标签
label the node	为节点打标签
label the image	为图像打标签

We do not label the topics, but when labels are needed, they can be suggested by domain experts.
我们并没有给话题打标签，但是如果需要，我们可以从领域专家那里取得。

Day 126

minimize
/ˈmɪnɪmaɪz/ v. 使……减少到最低

minimize the number	把数字降到最低
minimize the cost	把成本降到最低
minimize the time	把时间降到最少
minimize the error	把误差降到最少

Some may want to minimize task completion time at any cost, while others may want to minimize the cost and accept higher service delays.
有些人可能希望不惜一切代价减少完成任务需要的时间,而其他人可能想降低成本,愿意接受更长时间的服务延迟。

platform
/ˈplætfɔːm/ n. 平台

computing platform	计算平台
simulation platform	仿真平台
service platform	服务平台
software platform	软件平台

The user may have only a vague idea of how the program will behave on a given problem instance and computational platform.
用户可能只对项目在特定问题和计算平台上的表现有一个模糊的概念。

Day 127

identification
/aɪˌdentɪfɪˈkeɪʃn/ n. 识别

speaker identification	扬声器识别
biometric identification	生物识别
systematic identification	系统识别
feature identification	特征识别

We demonstrated the feasibility of such a method for large-scale speaker identification.
我们阐述了采用大规模扬声器识别的可行性。

transaction

/trænˈzækʃn/ *n.* 交易；买卖

transaction cost	交易成本
transaction processing	事物处理
transaction value	交易价值
transaction security	交易安全性
financial **transaction**	金融交易

For example, to prevent money laundering and other illegal financial transactions, the Internal Revenue Service in the U.S. requires financial organizations to report large monetary transactions.
例如，为了预防洗钱和其他非法金融交易，美国联邦税务局要求金融机构汇报大型货币交易。

Day 128

deployment

/dɪˈplɔɪmənt/ *n.* 有效运用；部署；调动

application **deployment**	应用部署
network **deployment**	网络部署
large-scale **deployment**	大规模部署
runtime **deployment**	运行部署
real-world **deployment**	实际部署

The first topology represents a private network deployment (e.g., enterprise network, single Internet service provider or campus network).
第一个拓扑学代表了私人网络部署(例如，企业网络、单一网络服务或校园网络)。

temporal

/ˈtempərəl/ *adj.* 时间的；暂时的

temporal information	时间信息
temporal resolution	时间分辨率
temporal planning	时间规划
temporal dynamics	时间动态
temporal constraints	时间约束

The adaptive temporal estimation using spatial-temporal information from neighboring nodes is much closer to the actual values.
借助临近节点时间空间信息的自适应时间估计更接近实际值。

Day 129

assignment

/əˈsaɪnmənt/ n. 赋值

task assignment	任务分配
truth assignment	真值指派
weight assignment	权重赋值
probability assignment	可信度分配；概率分配

The weight assignment and the similarity computation methods should be adapted to the ontology matching context.
我们应调整权重赋值和相似度计算方法以适应本体匹配情境。

convergence

/kənˈvɜːdʒəns/ n. 收敛

optimal convergence	最优收敛
service convergence	业务融合
first-order convergence	一阶收敛
exponential convergence	指数收敛
premature convergence	早熟收敛

Service convergence means managing services over a common networking platform to enable delivery of these services to customers using a common set of mechanisms.
业务融合指的是通过一个共同的网络平台管理业务，借助一套共同的机制为顾客提供服务。

Day 130

parallel
/ˈpærəlel/ *adj.* 平行的；并行的

parallel computing	并行计算
parallel path	平行路径
parallel search	并行搜索
parallel implementation	并行执行

Parallel computing provides an obvious source of performance improvement: if the work can be distributed over a number of processes then less time will be required to perform the simulation.
并行计算可以明显改善表现：如果我们可以把工作分配在几个不同过程中，那么所需模拟时间就会减少。

effectiveness
/ɪˈfektɪvnəs/ *n.* 有效性，效力

security effectiveness	安全有效性
retrieval effectiveness	检索效率
cost effectiveness	成本效益
system effectiveness	系统有效性

In particular, this paper is not looking for ways to improve security effectiveness.
尤其是本论文并不是在寻找改善安全有效性的方式。

Day 131

inference
/ˈɪnfərəns/ *n.* 推断；推论

sequential inference	顺序推理
statistical inference	统计推理
Bayesian inference	贝叶斯推理
extension inference	可拓推理

In Section 4, our decision theory is applied for a statistical inference problem.
在第四节中,我们的决策理论被用于一个统计推理问题。

anomaly

/əˈnɒməli/ n. 异常事物;反常现象;近点角;近点距离

anomaly detection	异常检测
anomaly diagnosis	异常诊断
anomaly detector	异常检测器
anomaly probability	异常概率

With the aim of illustrating practical examples of anomaly diagnosis components, this work selected some of the most influential efforts in this area.
为了阐释异常诊断构成的实际案例,本研究选取了领域中最有影响力的尝试。

Day 132

query

/ˈkwɪəri/ v. 询问;查询

query the sensor	查询传感器
query the deletion	查询删除
query the variable	查询变量
query the registry	查询注册表

This enables applications to query the sensor system for data/information using flexible content descriptors.
这使得应用能够采用灵活的内容描述符查询传感器系统。

monitor

/ˈmɒnɪtə(r)/ v. 监视;监听

monitor the progress	监测进展
monitor the performance	监测表现
monitor the network	监测网络
monitor the system	检测系统

Nodes in the network can indirectly monitor the performance of other nodes nearby.
网络中的节点可以简介监测临近其他节点的表现。

Day 133

filter
/ˈfɪltə(r)/ *n.* 过滤

bloom **filter**	布隆过滤器
Bayesian **filter**	贝叶斯滤波器
spam **filter**	垃圾邮件过滤器
heuristic **filter**	启发式过滤
median **filter**	中值滤波器

Examples of defense costs include: cost of security measures, such as spam filters and antivirus.
防御成本包括各种安全措施成本,例如垃圾邮件过滤器和杀毒软件。

simulate
/ˈsɪmjuleɪt/ *v.* 模拟

simulate the flow	模拟流程
simulate the behavior	模拟行为
simulate the effect	模拟效果
simulate the dynamic interaction	模拟动态互动

Data are used in specific ways to test the model's ability to simulate the system.
我们以特定方式使用数据检验模型模拟系统的能力。

Day 134

engine
/ˈendʒɪn/ *n.* 引擎

software **engine**	软件引擎
search **engine**	搜索引擎
reverse **engine**	反向引擎
feature **engine**	特征引擎
knowledge **engine**	知识引擎

The impact of this study on software engineers is two-fold.
本研究对软件引擎的影响是两方面的。

filter

/ˈfɪltə(r)/ *v.* 过滤

filter the uncertainty	过滤不确定性
filter the results	过滤结果
filter the information	过滤信息
filter the graph	过滤图表

With this formulation, the expected cost is the statistic used to filter the uncertainty.
有了这个公式，预期成本是过滤不确定性所需的数据。

Day 135

retrieval

/rɪˈtriːvl/ *n.* 提取；检索

information retrieval	信息提取
video retrieval	视频检索
image retrieval	图像检索
text retrieval	文本检索
code retrieval	代码检索

Organisations are increasingly using the Internet for information retrieval purposes.
机构越来越依赖互联网进行信息检索。

static

/ˈstætɪk/ *adj.* 静态的

static analysis	静态分析
static data	静态数据
static model	静态模型
static loading	静态载荷

Rutar et al. conducted a case study on five static analysis tools comparing their effectiveness.
鲁塔尔等人对五个静态分析工具进行了案例分析，比较它们的有效性。

Day 136

explicit

/ɪkˈsplɪsɪt/ *adj.* 清楚的；明白的

explicit representation	外显表征
explicit time	明确时间
explicit knowledge	显性知识
explicit metadata	明确元数据
explicit authentication	显性验证

Tasks with lower thresholds can be accomplished without an explicit authentication step.
阈值较低的任务可以不借助外显表征阶段验证。

mobile

/ˈməʊbaɪl/ *adj.* 移动的

mobile device	移动设备
mobile system	可移动系统
mobile application	移动应用程序
mobile node	移动节点
mobile network	移动网络

A mobile device user may offload code or data directly.
移动设备用户可以直接卸载代码或数据。

Day 137

signal

/ˈsɪɡnəl/ *n.* 信号；暗号；标志

| speech signal | 语言信号，语音信号 |
| acoustic signal | 声学信号 |

audio **signal**	音频信号
sensor **signal**	传感器信号
bluetooth **signal**	蓝牙信号

The speech signal is the fastest and the most natural method of communication between humans.
语音信号是人类之间交流最快、最自然的方式。

access

/ˈækses/ v. 进入；接入；获取

access the data	获取数据
access the service	访问服务
access the information	获取信息
access the application	获取应用
access the device	获取设备

In addition, a streaming data interface is provided which allows applications to access the data for analysis.
此外，流数据接口可以使应用获取数据进行分析。

Day 138

annotation

/ˌænəˈteɪʃn/ n. 注释；评注；注释；加注

semantic **annotation**	语义标注
manual **annotation**	手工标注
automatic **annotation**	自动标注
metadata **annotation**	元信息标注
document **annotation**	文档注释

A more detailed explanation of the general semantic annotation and querying process used here can be found.
关于此处的语义标注和检索过程，我们可以找到一个更详细的解释。

verify

/ˈverɪfaɪ/ v. 验证

verify the accuracy	验证准确性
verify the integrity	验证完整性
verify the suitability	验证适用性
verify the soundness	验证合理性

It is important for scientists to be able to verify the correctness of their own experiments, or to review the correctness of their peers' work.
对于科学家来说,验证自己试验的准确性或者回顾同伴试验的准确性至关重要。

Day 139

validity

/vəˈlɪdəti/ n. 有效性;效度

discriminant **validity**	区分效度
convergent **validity**	收敛效度
cluster **validity**	集群有效性
interaction **validity**	互动有效性

Table 5 results establish convergent and discriminant validity of the model constructs.
表 5 展示了模型结构的收敛效度和区分效度。

symbol

/ˈsɪmbl/ n. 符号;象征

symbol image	字符图像
symbol sequence	符号序列
symbol recognition	符号识别
symbol probability	符号概率

First, we evaluate the performance of the five classifier fusion methods for isolated symbol recognition using two different databases.
首先,我们使用两个不同的数据库评估了五个分类器融合方法在孤立符号识别上的表现。

Day 140

virtual

/ˈvɜːtʃuəl/ *adj.* 虚拟的；模拟的

virtual machine	虚拟机器
virtual friendship	虚拟友谊
virtual team	虚拟团队
virtual time	虚拟时间
virtual laboratory	虚拟实验室

In contrast, resource management games require the player to manage a virtual environment using limited resources.
相反，资源管理游戏需要使用有限资源管理虚拟环境。

adapt

/əˈdæpt/ *v.* 调整；适应；改编

adapt to the technologies	适应技术
adapt to the environment	适应环境
adapt to the interface	适应界面
adapt to the context	适应情境

Humans appear to adapt to the interface and learning algorithm.
人类似乎在适应界面和学习算法。

Day 141

locate

/ləʊˈkeɪt/ *v.* 定位；确定……的位置

locate the source	定位源头
locate the sensors	定位传感器

locate the position	定位位置
locate the cluster	定位集群

Visual system also includes a face tracker to locate the position of its human communication partner.
视觉系统同样包括一个能够定位人类交流伙伴的面部追踪器。

update

/ʌpˈdeɪt/ *n.* 更新；新型；新版

index update	索引更新
software update	软件更新
memory update	存储器更新
probability update	概率更新

If either implicit or explicit authentication is successful, the carrier enters the profile update phase.
不论成功的是隐性还是显性验证，载体都会进入配置文件更新阶段。

Day 142

verification

/ˌverɪfɪˈkeɪʃn/ *n.* 验证

formal verification	形式化验证
biometric verification	生物特征认证
identity verification	身份验证
semantic verification	语义验证
security verification	安全验证

Many ontology matching systems have integrated a semantic verification component.
许多本体匹配系统包含了语义验证的成分。

technical

/ˈteknɪk(ə)l/ *adj.* 技术性的

technical expertise	技术专长
technical detail	技术细节
technical staff	技术人员
technical knowledge	技术知识
technical aspect	技术方面

At each delegation stage, an employee with specialized responsibility and technical expertise interprets his or her assigned obligations.
在每一代表阶段,具有专业责任和技术知识的员工会解读指派给他/她的责任。

Day 143

root

/ruːt/ *n.* 根;(多项式方程的)根

square root	平方根
tree root	树根
root node	根节点
root vertex	根顶点
root bridge	根网桥

Another way to minimize the depth of the tree is to choose a root node at the center of graph.
另一个把树深度降到最低的方法是选择图中央的一个根节点。

loop

/luːp/ *n.* 循环

feedback loop	反馈回路
outer loop	外层循环
while loop	while 循环
inner loop	内循环
main loop	主循环

Another unique feature of our prototype is the combination of crowdsourcing with machine listening, and the feedback loop between algorithms and humans.
我们模型的另一个特征是将众包、机听以及算法和人之间的反馈循环结合在了一起。

Day 144

adaptive
/əˈdæptɪv/ *adj.* 适应的；有适应能力的

adaptive method	自适应法；适配法
adaptive algorithm	自适应算法
adaptive refinement	自适应精化
adaptive management	适应性管理
adaptive sampling	自适应抽样

Furthermore, it provides adaptive sampling techniques for global and local refinement.
此外，它为全球和局部精化提供适应性采样技术。

scope
/skəʊp/ *n.* 作用域；范围

project scope	项目范围
research scope	研究范围
geographic scope	地理范围
limited scope	范围有限
specific scope	特定范围

Indeed, one threat is the very specific scope of this unique case study.
诚然，其中一个威胁就是这一独特案例研究的特定范围。

Day 145

mode
/məʊd/ *n.* 模式；样式

experiment mode	试验模式
single-threaded mode	单线程模式
search mode	搜索模式

multi-threaded **mode**	多线程模式
concurrent **mode**	并发模式

When an engine is run in single-threaded mode, our observations were that its evaluations for moves were identical over multiple runs.
当引擎以单线程模式工作,我们观察到多次运行中多个步骤的评价十分相似。

likelihood

/ˈlaɪklihʊd/ n. 可能性;似然

maximum **likelihood**	最大似然
log **likelihood**	对数似然
marginal **likelihood**	边缘相似性
conditional **likelihood**	条件似然

Maximum Likelihood Estimates (MLE) were used for construct estimation.
人们将最大相似估计用于构建评估。

Day 146

equivalent

/ɪˈkwɪvələnt/ adj. 相等的;相同的

equivalent number	同等数量
equivalent polynomials	等价多项式
equivalent equation	等价方程
equivalent version	相同版本
equivalent result	相同结果

The choice of any of these fitness functions leads to equivalent results.
选择任何适应度函数都会产生相同的结果。

computing

/kəmˈpjuːtɪŋ/ n. 计算;处理

cloud **computing**	云计算
parallel **computing**	并行计算
performance **computing**	性能计算

scientific **computing**	科学计算
distributed **computing**	分布式计算

These issues have already been the subject of research in the distributed computing community.
这些问题已经成为分布式计算社区的研究对象。

Day 147

allocation
/ˌæləˈkeɪʃn/ *n.* 分配(物);分派

resource **allocation**	资源分配
bandwidth **allocation**	带宽分配
memory **allocation**	内存分配
water **allocation**	水资源分配

Well-validated predictive tools for forest fire risk would be useful for resource allocation.
经过充分验证的森林火险预测工具对资源分配十分有用。

valid
/ˈvælɪd/ *adj.* 有效的

valid symbol	有效象征
valid path	有效路径
valid tag	有效标签
valid value	有效值

A state transition indicates a valid path between two resources.
状态转变暗示了两种资源之间的有效路径。

Day 148

center
/ˈsentə(r)/ *n.* 中心;中央

data **center**	数据中心
cluster **center**	簇中心,聚类中心,团中心
scattering **center**	散射中心
resource **center**	资源中心

Our work draws upon recent advances in virtual machines and dynamic provisioning in data centers.
我们的研究基于数据中心虚拟机器和动态准备金的最新进展展开。

learning
/ˈlɜːnɪŋ/ *n.* 学习

supervised **learning**	监督学习
unsupervised **learning**	无监督学习
reinforcement **learning**	强化学习
active **learning**	主动学习

The advantage of supervised learning methods is that the annotation of training data can be carried out in such a way that all relationships and concepts are selected to meet the needs of the selected domain or application.
监督学习方法的优势是训练数据的标注中选取的关系和概念都可以满足特定领域和应用的需要。

Day 149

library
/ˈlaɪbrəri/ *n.* 程序库

model **library**	模型库
digital **library**	数字图书馆
component **library**	组件库
software **library**	软件库

In this paper, we presented a new methodology for watershed modeling based on a knowledge library and a machine learning approach.
本论文中,我们基于知识图书馆和机器学习方法为流域模型展示了新方法。

usage

/ˈjuːsɪdʒ/ *n.* 使用

memory **usage**	内存使用
resource **usage**	资源利用率;资源使用
bandwidth **usage**	带宽利用
service **usage**	业务用途

Both run-time and memory usage results for both techniques are shown in Fig. 5.
两种技术的程序运行期和内存使用结构都展示在了图5中。

Day 150

utility

/juːˈtɪləti/ *n.* 功用;效用

transferable **utility**	可转移效用
expected **utility**	期望效用
transfer **utility**	转移效用
societal **utility**	社会效用

Expected utility theory is based on the notion that people choose options that provide the most benefit.
预期效用理论背后的概念是人们会做出利益最大化的选择。

format

/ˈfɔːmæt/ *n.* 格式化;格式

data **format**	数据格式
standard **format**	标准格式
document **format**	文档格式
readable **format**	可读格式

This data format is more compact and it is very common in scientific data.
这种数据格式更简练且在科学数据中更为常见。

Day 151

continuous

/kənˈtɪnjuəs/ *adj.* 连续不断的；持续的

continuous function	连续函数
continuous variable	连续变量
continuous monitoring	持续监控
continuous integration	持续集成

We can now conduct the same complex computing with continuous variables.
我们现在可以采用连续变量进行相同的复杂计算。

automated

/ˈɔːtəmeɪtɪd/ *adj.* 自动的

automated reasoning	自动推理
automated tool	自动化工具
automated response	自动响应
automated testing	自动化测试

The automated approach does not pre-judge whether the feature is likely to be useful for classification.
自动化方法并不预先判定哪个特征对分类最为有用。

Day 152

hierarchy

/ˈhaɪərɑːki/ *n.* 等级制度；统治集团；等级体系

class hierarchy	类层次结构
analytical hierarchy	层次分析法

location **hierarchy**	位置层次结构
role **hierarchy**	角色层次;角色继承
static **hierarchy**	静态层次结构

In this section different steps of the proposed evaluation hierarchy are illustrated along with examples.
本节中提出的评价等级不同步骤配有案例。

binary

/ˈbaɪnəri/ n. 二进制

binary search	二分查找
binary decision	二元决策
binary variable	二进制变量
binary output	二进制输出
binary tree	二叉树

For some collections of constraints, various types of searches may be used for identifying whether the constraints are consistent. For example, a binary search may be used.
对于一些限制,我们可以采用各式各样的查找方法来判断这些限制是否一致。例如,我们可以采用二分查找法。

Day 153

triangle

/ˈtraɪæŋgl/ n. 三角;三角形

golden **triangle**	金三角
arbitrary **triangle**	任意三角形
equilateral **triangle**	等边三角形
triangle inequality	三角不等式

Its outline roughly forms an equilateral triangle.
它的大致轮廓是一个等边三角形。

precision

/prɪˈsɪʒn/ *n.* 精确性；准确性

average **precision**	平均精度
learning **precision**	学习精密
machine **precision**	机器精度
double **precision**	双精度

The mean of these average precision values is calculated.
我们计算出了平均准确度均值。

Day 154

feedback

/ˈfiːdbæk/ *n.* 反馈意见；(信号返回电子音响系统所致的)噪声；(返回机器、系统或者程序的)返回信息，返回电流

feedback control	反馈控制
feedback loop	反馈循环
feedback mechanism	反馈机制
feedback information	反馈信息

A feedback loop is the name given to a set of relationships where one variable leads to a change in another variable that eventually leads to a change in the original variable.
反馈循环指的是不同变量之间的关系，一个变量的变化会引起另一个变量的变化，最终导致初始变量的变化。

uniform

/ˈjuːnɪfɔːm/ *adj.* 相同的；统一的

uniform distribution	均匀分布
uniform source	均匀源
uniform interface	统一接口，一致接口
uniform distribution	均布载荷

Every single resource in Fig. 5 (e.g., model, inputs) exposes the same uniform interface.
图 5 中的单一资源展示了统一界面。

Day 155

segment
/ˈseɡmənt/ n. 部分；片段

image **segment**	影像片段
road **segment**	道路段
network **segment**	网络段
motion **segment**	运动片段

It can be seen that only a very small percentage of the motion segments remain.
我们可以看到，运动片段只保留了很少一部分。

violation
/ˌvaɪəˈleɪʃn/ n. 违背；违反；侵权行为

security **violation**	安全违规
constraint **violation**	约束违反
threshold **violation**	阈值违反

In this section, we review related work in security and legal requirements research, industry and legal analysis of security violations.
本节我们回顾了安全和法律要求研究的相关著作，以及安全违规的行业和法律分析。

Day 156

depth
/depθ/ n. 深度

search **depth**	搜索深度
water **depth**	水深
penetration **depth**	穿透深度
layer **depth**	混合层深度

As the search depth increases, the relevance of the evaluation made at the leaf nodes decreases.
随着搜索深度的增加，叶子节点处评价相关性降低。

catchment

/ˈkætʃmənt/ *n.* 集水；流域

catchment area	集水区
catchment hydrology	流域水文
catchment characteristics	流域特征
catchment sediment	流域泥沙
catchment outlet	集水出口

A relationship between the model sensitivity to these parameters and the catchment area was also apparent.
模型对这些参数敏感度和集水区之间的关系同样明显。

Day 157

overlay

/ˌəʊvəˈleɪ/ *v.* 覆盖

overlay path	重叠路径
overlay node	重叠节点
overlay network	覆盖网络

There are multiple reasons for using a multi-hop overlay path.
使用多点跳跃重叠通路背后有许多原因。

magnitude

/ˈmæɡnɪtjuːd/ *n.* 巨大；重要性

gradient magnitude	梯度幅值
velocity magnitude	速度大小
error magnitude	误差大小,误差值
varying magnitude	变化幅度

For each pixel in the action region, we encode the gradient magnitudes and orientations in its spatiotemporal 3D space.
对于活动区域中的每一个像素，我们为 3D 时空的梯度幅值和方向编码。

Day 158

aggregation
/ˌæɡrɪˈɡeɪʃn/ *n.* 聚集体；集合体

data **aggregation**	数据聚合
spatial **aggregation**	空间集聚，空间聚集

To alleviate broadcast storms, this work has focused on data aggregation based on distance from the source.
为了缓解广播风暴，这部作品基于源头距离关注数据聚合。

minimal
/ˈmɪnɪml/ *adj.* 极小的；极少的

minimal model	极小模型
minimal processing	最小过程
minimal length	最小长度
minimal impact	最小影响

The sequence of minimal cost which transforms one graph into another.
最低成本序列将一个图表转换为另一个图表。

Day 159

projection
/prəˈdʒekʃn/ *n.* 预测；投影

climate **projection**	气候预测
normal **projection**	正轴投影
linear **projection**	线性投影
image **projection**	图像投影

Texture features of face and palmprint are extracted separately and then a linear projection scheme.
面部和掌纹特征首先被单独提取出来，然后进行线性投影。

prototype

/ˈprəʊtətaɪp/ n. 原型

prototype implementation	原型实现
prototype theory	原型理论
prototype system	原型系统
prototype software	原型软件
prototype data	原型数据

Consequently, the label semantics approach can be applied to both variants of prototype theory.
因此,标签语义方法可以用于原型理论的两个变体。

Day 160

extraction

/ɪkˈstrækʃn/ n. 提取;提出

feature **extraction**	特征提取
function **extraction**	函数提取
data **extraction**	数据提取
information **extraction**	信息提取
watermark **extraction**	水印提取

This attack interferes with the feature extraction routines to manipulate or provide false data for further processing.
这种袭击干扰特征提取路径,操控或提供错误数据,阻碍继续运行。

filtering

/ˈfɪltərɪŋ/ n. 过滤,滤除

spam **filtering**	垃圾邮件过滤
Bayesian **filtering**	贝叶斯过滤
dynamic **filtering**	动态滤波器;动态筛选
information **filtering**	信息过滤
semantic **filtering**	语义过滤

The appliance is likely to contain optimized hardware for spam filtering.
这一设备可能包含垃圾邮件过滤优化软件。

Day 161

tagging
/ˈtæɡɪŋ/ n. 标注

social **tagging**	社会化标注
POS tagging	词性标注
automated **tagging**	自动标记
semantic **tagging**	语义标注
concept **tagging**	概念标注

The authors investigate the impact of the specific characteristics of tweets on several text preprocessing steps: language identification, tokenization, POS tagging and named entity recognition.
作者调查了推特在文本加工方面的许多特征：语言识别、分词、词性标注和命名实体识别。

pseudo
/ˈsuːdəʊ/ adj. 假的；伪装的

pseudo code	伪代码
pseudo random	伪随机
pseudo test	伪测验
pseudo time	拟时间
pseudo address	伪地址

The pseudo code of algorithm is outlined in Fig. 4.
伪代码算法出现在图 4 中。

Day 162

validate
/ˈvælɪdeɪt/ v. 验证

validate the effectiveness	验证有效性
validate the results	验证结果
validate the performance	验证表现
validate the model	验证模型
validate the security	验证安全性

To validate the effectiveness of the proposed method, we performed two kinds of experiments: face recognition and facial expression recognition.
为了验证提出方法的有效性,我们进行了两种实验:人脸识别和面部表情识别。

malicious

/məˈlɪʃəs/ *adj.* 恶意的

malicious software	恶意软件
malicious node	恶意节点
malicious code	恶意代码
malicious attack	恶意袭击
malicious user	恶意用户

Usually only sites that are suspected of installing malicious software are kept in the database.
通常数据库中只包含了可能会安装恶意软件的网站。

Day 163

robot

/ˈrəʊbɒt/ *n.* 机器人

mobile **robot**	移动机器人
autonomous **robot**	自主机器人
delivery **robot**	送货机器人
two-wheeled **robot**	两轮机器人
simulated **robot**	模拟机器人

The experimental set up consists of a wireless network incorporating mobile robots, robot simulators, and distributed sensors.
实验装置中的无线网络包括移动机器人、机器人仿真器和分布式传感器。

deploy

/dɪˈplɔɪ/ v. 部署,调动;利用

deploy the environment	部署环境
deploy the software	部署软件
deploy the response	部署回应
deploy the monitor	部署监视器

We are not able to deploy the environment.
我们无法部署环境。

Day 164

evolution

/ˌiːvəˈluːʃn/ n. 演化;进展

schema evolution	模式演变
differential evolution	差分进化
interactive evolution	交互进化;互动演化
technological evolution	技术演化

A complementary explanation for this shift in focus includes the changes in threat scenarios based upon technological evolution, such as the shift towards increasingly interconnected corporate networks.
对这种焦点转变的补充解释包括基于技术演化的威胁情境变化,例如公司网络的联系越来越紧密。

discrete

/dɪˈskriːt/ adj. 分离的;个别的

discrete time	离散时间
discrete event	离散事件
discrete system	离散系统,集块参数系统
discrete value	离散值

In this example, we solve a discrete system of size.
在本案例中,我们解决了一个离散系统规模的问题。

Day 165

plot

/plɒt/ n. 图表

sample **plot**	样本图
scatter **plot**	散点图
box **plot**	箱线图
residual **plot**	残差图

Analyses were supplemented by residual plots.
我们的分析中补充了残差图。

highlight

/ˈhaɪlaɪt/ v. 强调；突出

highlight the importance	强调重要性
highlight the fact	强调事实
highlight the practical performance	强调实际表现
highlight the strengths	强调优势

We explore the design of such a resource-oriented solution in detail, suggest some implementation strategies, and highlight the importance of using uniform interfaces.
我们详细探索了这一资源导向性解决方案，提出了一些实施策略，强调了使用统一界面的重要性。

Day 166

monitoring

/ˈmɒnɪtərɪŋ/ n. 监视；监督

probabilistic **monitoring**	概率监控
network **monitoring**	网络监控；网络监视
quality **monitoring**	质量监控
project **monitoring**	项目监控；项目监测；工程监测

For active traffic monitoring, the primary mechanism is the probe message.
对于主动交通监测来说,最主要的机制是探测消息。

exact
/ɪɡˈzækt/ *adj.* 确切的

exact solution	确切解决方案
exact value	确切值
exact number	确切数字
exact model	确切模型

No exact solution is available; no exact value of the critical parameter is available either.
既无法获得确切的解决方案,关键参数也没有确切值。

Day 167

regression
/rɪˈɡreʃn/ *n.* 回归

linear regression	线性回归
logistic regression	逻辑回归
multiple regression	多元回归
stepwise regression	逐步回归
multivariate regression	多元回归

We used the multiple linear regression model, the standard statistical technique for modelling and analyzing several variables.
我们使用了多重线性回归模型,建模和分析多个变量的标准统计策略。

Gaussian
/ˈɡaʊsɪən/ *adj.* 高斯的

Gaussian noise	高斯噪声
Gaussian kernel	高斯核
Gaussian distribution	高斯分布
Gaussian mixture	高斯混合
Gaussian quadrature	高斯求积

As the Gaussian noise level increases, better results are achieved.
随着高斯噪声水平的提高,我们得到了更好的结果。

Day 168

propagation
/ˌprɒpəˈɡeɪʃn/ n. (运动、光线、声音等的)传送

wave propagation	波传播
similarity propagation	相似度传播
crack propagation	裂纹扩展
worm propagation	蠕虫病毒传播

In this section we briefly recall the main equations of structural vibrations and of wave propagation.
本节我们简要回顾了结构振动的主要等式和波传播。

authorization
/ˌɔːθəraɪˈzeɪʃn/ n. 批准;授权

conceptual authorization	概念授权
distributed authorization	分布式授权
authorization model	授权模型
authorization infrastructure	授权基础设施
authorization strategy	授权策略

The authorization model is based on role-based access control.
授权模型是基于角色的访问控制。

Day 169

prior
/ˈpraɪə(r)/ adj. 先前的;事先的

prior research	先前研究
prior work	先前的工作
prior knowledge	先验知识
prior probability	先验概率
prior distribution	先验分布

Prior research in information processing shows that men and women differ in the way they internalize information stimulation and respond.
先前信息处理研究表明，男性和女性在内化信息刺激和回应上有所不同。

bound

/baʊnd/ *v.* 绑定；约束

bound the number	绑定数字
bound the sample	绑定样本
bound the algorithm	约束算法

Another promising avenue of future research is to bound the number.
另一个未来研究的方向是绑定数字。

Day 170

read

/riːd/ *v.* 读取

read the data	读取数据
read the policy	读取政策
read the question	读取问题

It could read the data and then forward it on to the intended destination.
它可以读取数据并把数据传送到指定地点。

retrieve

/rɪˈtriːv/ *v.* 提取

retrieve the information	提取信息
retrieve the website	提取网页
retrieve the resource	提取资源

The information is retrieved within a certain period of time.
信息在特定时间提取出来。

Day 171

guarantee

/ˌgærənˈtiː/ v. 确保；保证

guarantee the stability	确保稳定性
guarantee the success	确保成功
guarantee the reliability	确保可靠性

We need to guarantee the stability of our evaluation results.
我们需要确保评价结果的稳定性。

eliminate

/ɪˈlɪmɪneɪt/ v. 消除

eliminate the need	消除需求
eliminate the probability	排除概率
eliminate the instability	排除不稳定性

We need a special algorithm to eliminate the instability.
我们需要一种特殊算法来排除不稳定性。

Day 172

overview

/ˈəʊvəvjuː/ n. 概述；综述

comprehensive **overview**	全面概述
detailed **overview**	详细概述
broad **overview**	宽泛概述

In this paper we give a comprehensive overview of the algorithm.
本论文中我们对算法进行了详细概述。

probabilistic

/ˌprɒbəˈlɪstɪk/ *adj.* 概率性的

probabilistic model	概率模型
probabilistic search	概率搜索
probabilistic design	概率设计
probabilistic framework	概率框架
probabilistic theory	概率理论

Another technique to solve probabilistic planning problems is replanning.
解决概率规划问题的另一个策略是重新规划。

Day 173

template

/ˈtempleɪt/ *n.* 模板；样板

biometric **template**	生物模板
entity **template**	实体模板
sentence **template**	句子模板

Entity templates can be arranged into inheritance trees.
实体模板可以以继承树的形式呈现。

segmentation

/ˌsegmenˈteɪʃn/ *n.* 分割

image **segmentation**	图像分割
texture **segmentation**	纹理分割
segmentation result	分割结果
segmentation accuracy	分割精度
segmentation problem	分割问题

Recently, a comparative evaluation of four interactive segmentation algorithms is reported.
近期报告中比较了四项互动分割算法。

Day 174

list
/lɪst/ v. 把……列入清单

list the number	列出数字
list the value	列出值
list the term	列出术语

For each topic, we list the number of works that focus on it, either directly or indirectly.
对于每一个话题,我们列出了直接或间接重点研究。

robust
/rəʊˈbʌst/ adj. 强壮的;强有力的

robust control	鲁棒控制
robust controller	鲁棒控制器
robust algorithm	鲁棒算法
robust modeling	鲁棒建模;稳健建模

One of its main objectives is to estimate mathematical models that are suitable for high performance robust control design techniques.
其中一个主要目的是为高性能鲁棒控制设计技术预估数学模型。

Day 175

theoretical
/ˌθɪəˈretɪk(ə)l/ adj. 理论的;假设的

theoretical framework	理论框架
theoretical model	理论模型
theoretical analysis	理论分析
theoretical results	理论结果
theoretical basis	理论偏见

We need to provide a theoretical framework for comparing systems and designing new ones.
我们需要为比较系统和设计新系统提供一个理论框架。

appendix

/əˈpendɪks/ *n.* 附录

theorem **appendix**	定理附录
definition **appendix**	定义附录

Please refer to the theorem appendix.
请参见定理附录。

Day 176

priority

/praɪˈɒrəti/ *n.* 优先事项；优先权

default **priority**	默认优先级
overall **priority**	整体优先级
group **priority**	团队优先
first **priority**	首要优先事项

They're either assigned to this project or available as a first priority.
它们或是分配给了这个项目，或是作为最高优先事项。

polynomial

/ˌpɒliˈnəʊmiəl/ *n./ adj.* 多项式的；多项式

polynomial time	多项式时间
polynomial kernel	多项式核
polynomial parameter	多项式参数
polynomial order	多项式阶数
polynomial space	多项式空间

In our work, we employed a polynomial kernel to project the data on to the kernel space.
在我们的研究中，我们采用多项式内核把数据投射到多项式空间中。

Day 177

processor

/ˈprəʊsesə(r)/ n. 处理器；处理机

multiple **processor**	多处理器
single **processor**	单处理机
element **processor**	元件处理机

The second approach used multiple processors where each process writes to their own file.
第二个方法使用多重处理器，把每个进程写入自己的文件。

integrated

/ˈɪntɪɡreɪtɪd/ adj. 综合的

integrated assessment	综合评价
integrated modeling	综合模型
integrated approach	综合方法
integrated system	集成系统

The achievements of integrated assessment modelling are highlighted.
人们强调了综合评价模型的成就。

Day 178

indicator

/ˈɪndɪkeɪtə(r)/ n. 指示器；显示器；指标

performance **indicator**	绩效指标
component **indicator**	成分指标
multiple **indicator**	多重指标

This requires knowledge of the domain coupled with the ability to identify patterns involving multiple indicators.
这需要相关领域的知识和识别多重指标的能力。

generic

/dʒəˈnerɪk/ *adj.* 一般的；通用的

generic model	通用模型
generic framework	通用框架
generic algorithm	泛型算法；通用算法
generic query	通用查询
generic mechanisms	通用机制

We suggest that a generic model is a useful starting position for understanding the complex interplay between relevant constructs out of which more focused research studies may be designed.
我们建议可以以一个通用模型作为有用的起点，理解不同概念之间的相互作用，进而设计重点更为突出的研究。

Day 179

metadata

/ˈmetədeɪtə/ *n.* 元信息；元数据

additional metadata	额外的元信息
relevant metadata	相关元信息
textual metadata	文本元信息
semantically-encoded metadata	经过语义编码的元信息
metadata acquisition	元数据采集

We process the textual metadata using an instance of Wikipedia Miner.
我们采用维基百科数据挖掘器加工文本元信息。

bias

/ˈbaɪəs/ *n.* 偏压；偏磁；偏移；移位

model bias	模型偏差
anchoring bias	锚定偏误
selection bias	选择偏见
non-response bias	无反应偏差
method bias	方法偏差

The lack of any "general factor" in the data also indicates a lack of any common method bias.
数据中缺乏一般因素也暗示其中缺乏任何共同方法偏差。

Day 180

code

/kəʊd/ v. 把……编码;把……译成密码;(给计算机)编写指令

code the message	为信息编码
code the watchlist	为监视列表编码
code the vector	为向量编码
code the test	为测试编码
code the system	为系统编码

The languages used to code the semantic descriptions may vary from application to application.
给语义描述编码的语言可能因应用而不同。

generalize

/ˈdʒenrəlaɪz/ v. 概括,归纳;推广,普及;笼统地表达

generalize the results	概括结果
generalize the model	概括模型
generalize the findings	概括发现
generalize the algorithm	概括算法
generalize the method	概括方法

We generalized the results based on this model.
我们基于这一模型概括结果。

Day 181

structural

/ˈstrʌktʃərəl/ adj. 结构上的;构造上的

structural properties	结构特征
structural parameters	结构参数
structural information	结构信息
structural refinement	结构优化
structural model	结构模型

The structural parameters are not assumed and will be random variables in the inversion process.
结构参数并不是既定的,在转换过程中会成为随机变量。

scale
/skeɪl/ *v.* 改变尺寸大小;按一定比例调节

scale the size	调节尺寸
scale the results	调整结果
scale the performance	调整性能

The min-max score normalization method was applied to scale the results of each technique.
最大最小分数归一化方法用于调节每种策略的结果。

Day 182

decomposition
/ˌdiːkɒmpəˈzɪʃn/ *n.* 分解

domain **decomposition**	域分解;[流]区域分解
tree **decomposition**	树分解
value **decomposition**	值分解
variance **decomposition**	方差分解
threshold **decomposition**	阈值分解

To calculate the rank of the matrix, we use Singular Value Decomposition (SVD).
为了计算矩阵的秩次,我们采用了单一值分解。

availability
/əˌveɪləˈbɪləti/ *n.* 可用性;可得性

data **availability**	数据可用性
resource **availability**	资源可用性
moisture **availability**	水分有效性
information **availability**	信息可得性
network **availability**	网络可用性

The first sort includes factors like strategy and planning, resource availability, and deployment quality.
第一类包含策略和规划、资源可用性和部署质量几个因素。

Day 183

hybrid

/ˈhaɪbrɪd/ *adj.* 混合的

hybrid approach	混合方法
hybrid model	混合模型
hybrid representation	混合表示
hybrid system	混合系统

The hybrid approach proposed in this paper combines multiple aspects.
本文中提出的混合方法融合了多个方面。

sampling

/ˈsɑːmplɪŋ/ *n.* 取样;抽样

adaptive **sampling**	自适应抽样
random **sampling**	随机抽样
uniform **sampling**	均匀取样
theoretical **sampling**	理论抽样
sequence **sampling**	序列抽样

Uniform random sampling ensures global reliability of the method.
统一抽样确保了方法的整体可靠性。

Day 184

stable
/ˈsteɪbl/ *adj.* 稳定的；牢固的

stable model	稳定模型
stable extension	稳定扩展
stable system	稳定系统
stable pattern	稳定模式

Typical anomalies can be detected timely, based on a stable system model.
基于稳定的系统模型，我们可以及时检测到典型异常。

quantitative
/ˈkwɒntɪtətɪv/ *adj.* 量化的

quantitative data	量化数据
quantitative evaluation	定量评估
quantitative analysis	量化分析
quantitative measure	量化措施
quantitative comparison	量化比较

This section provides a brief description of the qualitative and quantitative data collected during the experimental run.
本节简要描述了试验运转中收集到的质性和量化数据。

Day 185

nonlinear
/ˌnɒnˈlɪniə(r)/ *adj.* 非线性的

nonlinear elasticity	非线性弹性
nonlinear solver	非线性求解器
nonlinear wave	非线性波动，非线性波
nonlinear problem	非线性问题
nonlinear system	非线性系统

We begin by describing the variational formulation of the nonlinear elasticity problem.
我们首先会描述非线性弹性问题的变分公式化问题。

Markov

/ˈmarkɔf/ *n.* 马尔可夫

Markov chain	马尔可夫链
Markov model	马尔可夫模型
Markov decision	马尔可夫决策
Markov network	马尔可夫网络
Markov property	马尔可夫特性

Actually, the hidden Markov model framework is well suited to capture the temporal dynamics of dialog acts.
事实上,隐马尔可夫模型非常适合捕捉对话行为的时间动态。

Day 186

modification

/ˌmɒdɪfɪˈkeɪʃn/ *n.* 修改;修饰

modification program	修改程序
modification process	修改过程
modification approach	修改方法
modification strategies	修改策略

As a result, the query modification process might somehow reduce the interactive nature of a system.
因此,检索修改程序可能在某种程度上减弱系统的互动性。

interpolation

/ɪnˌtɜːpəˈleɪʃn/ *n.* 插入;篡改;填写;插值

polynomial **interpolation**	多项式插值
spatial **interpolation**	空间内插,空间插值
quadratic **interpolation**	二次插值,二次插值法

| nonlinear **interpolation** | 非线性插值 |
| adaptive **interpolation** | 自适应插值 |

The simplest way to find the unknown solution is to use the linear interpolation.
找到未知解决方案最简单的途径是使用线性插值。

Day 187

notation
/nəʊˈteɪʃn/ *n.* 标记系统；标记法

graphical **notation**	图形标记法
matrix **notation**	矩阵符号，矩阵记号
standard **notation**	标准计数法，标准符号表示法
model **notation**	模型符号

Throughout this work we use standard notation of probability theory.
整个研究中，我们使用的是概率理论标准计数法。

recall
/rɪˈkɔːl/ *n.* 召回

recall value	召回值
recall measure	召回措施
recall results	召回结果
recall statistics	召回数据

We find that increasing the period of change data does not improve recall values.
我们发现，延长变换数据的时间间隔并不会改善召回值。

Day 188

diagram
/ˈdaɪəɡræm/ *n.* 图表；图解

relationship diagram	关系图
phase diagram	相图
interaction diagram	交互图
transition diagram	推移图

The relationship diagram method simplified complicated problems into several major points.
关系图方法把复杂问题简化为几个要点。

calibration

/ˌkælɪˈbreɪʃn/ *n.* 标定；校准

calibration period	校正区间
calibration parameter	校准参数
calibration result	校准结果
calibration process	校准过程
calibration problem	校准问题

Simulation times can range from a few seconds to several minutes depending on the size of the modeled region and the length of time in the calibration period.
依据模拟区域大小和校准时间长短的不同，模拟时间可以从数秒延续到数分钟。

Day 189

track

/træk/ *v.* 追踪；追寻

track the interface	追踪界面
track the location	追踪地点
track the movement	追踪运动
track the vertices	追踪顶点
track the time	追踪时间

These systems are used to track the movement of tagged objects.
这些系统用于追踪标记物体。

email

/ˈiːmeɪl/ *n.* 电子邮件

email address	电子邮件地址
email message	电子邮件信息
email communication	电子邮件交流
email system	电子邮件系统
email data	电子邮件数据

We were mining data from a commercial repository where challenges related to contributors' multiple email addresses.
我们正在从一个商业数据库中挖掘数据,贡献者的多个电子邮件地址给我们带来了挑战。

Day 190

implication

/ˌɪmplɪˈkeɪʃn/ *n.* 含义

theoretical implication	理论含义
social implication	社会含义
profound implication	深远含义
long-term implication	长期含义

Economic research primarily emphasizes the theoretical implications of switching costs on market share and competition.
经济研究主要强调的是把成本转化为市场份额和竞争的理论含义。

runtime

/ˈrʌntaɪm/ *n.* 执行时间;运行时间

runtime performance	运行时性能
runtime plan	运行计划
runtime prediction	运行时预测
runtime analysis	运行分析
runtime security	运行安全

Its runtime performance is also an issue when data size is large.
当数据量较大时,运行表现同样构成问题。

Day 191

motivation
/ˌməʊtɪˈveɪʃn/ *n.* 动力;诱因;动机

primary **motivation**	主要动机
intrinsic **motivation**	内在动机
users **motivation**	用户动机
theoretical **motivation**	理论动机

The primary motivation for using hypothetical scenarios was to prevent social desirability bias.
使用假设情景的主要动机是避免社会期望偏见。

hierarchical
/ˌhaɪəˈrɑːkɪkl/ *adj.* 分等级的;等级制度的

hierarchical protection	分层保护
hierarchical clustering	层次聚类
hierarchical structure	分层结构
hierarchical path	分层路径
hierarchical refinement	分层细化

The hierarchical structure of tags can be used to determine the relevance.
标签的层次结构可以决定相关性。

Day 192

metric
/ˈmetrɪk/ *adj.* 度量的;公制的

metric system	公制系统
metric data	度量数据
metric analysis	计量分析
metric techniques	度量技术

It is important to assess the performance and security of any biometric system in order to identify and prevent threats.
为了识别和预防威胁,评估任何生物识别系统的表现和安全性至关重要。

manipulation
/məˈnɪpjuˈleɪʃn/ n. (对储存在计算机上的信息的)操作;处理

optimal **manipulation**	最优操作
data **manipulation**	数据操作
experimental **manipulation**	实验操作
functional **manipulation**	功能操纵

Users can incorporate geospatial data manipulation functions in the mappings.
用户可以在映射中纳入地理空间数据操纵功能。

Day 193

workflow
/ˈwɜːkfləʊ/ n. 工作流;工作流程

implementation **workflow**	实现工作流
scientific **workflow**	科学工作流程,科学工作流
workflow execution	工作流执行
workflow engine	工作流引擎
workflow system	工作流系统

The Grid Space virtual laboratory workflow system consists of two important parts to automatically run and manage workflows.
网格空间虚拟实验室工作流系统有两个重要组成部分,可自动运行和管理工作流。

transmission
/trænzˈmɪʃn/ n. (无线电、电视等信号)播送;发送

| data **transmission** | 数据传输 |
| message **transmission** | 信息传输 |

packet **transmission**	包传输；群发送；报文分组通信
fixed **transmission**	固定传输
network **transmission**	网络传输

We define a user as an individual with a fixed or mobile device that has wired or wireless data transmission capabilities and access to the Internet.
我们将用户定义为拥有固定或移动设备的个体，这些设备拥有有线或无线数据传输的功能并且可以上网。

Day 194

wireless

/ˈwaɪələs/ *adj.* 无线的

wireless node	无线节点
wireless network	无线网络
wireless sensor	无线传感器
wireless medium	无线介质
wireless communication	无线通信

Wireless communication systems in NGN will integrate different network access technologies such as WLAN.
下一代网络无线通信系统将包含不同的网络访问技术，例如无线局域网。

visual

/ˈvɪʒuəl/ *adj.* 视觉的

visual feedback	视觉反馈
visual representation	视觉呈现
visual paradigm	视觉范式
visual data	视觉数据
visual inspection	目视检查

We investigate the use of context-based visual feedback recognition.
我们考察了基于情景的视觉反馈识别。

Day 195

indices
/ˈɪndɪsiːz/ n. 指教；目录

sensitivity indices	灵敏度指标，灵敏度指数
meteorological indices	气象指数
connectivity indices	连通性指数
validity indices	效度指标
modification indices	修改指标

Many more complex meteorological indices depend on windspeed as an input.
许多复杂的气象指数依赖风速作为输入。

consistency
/kənˈsɪstənsi/ n. 一致性，连贯性；平滑度

internal consistency	内部一致性
data consistency	数据一致性
variable consistency	变量一致性
semantic consistency	语义一致性

There are strong data consistency requirements between the different policy management sites.
不同政策管理网站的数据一致性要求很高。

Day 196

integer
/ˈɪntɪdʒə(r)/ n. 整数；完整物；统一体

positive integer	正整数
non-negative integer	非负整数

integer linear programming	整数线性规划
integer value	整数值
integer encoding	整数编码

Constraint Integer Programming（CIP）is a novel paradigm that integrates Constraint Programming（CP），Mixed Integer Programming（MIP）and Satisfiability（SAT）modeling.
约束整数规划是一种全新的范式，融合了约束规划、混合整数规划和可满足性建模。

competitive

/kəmˈpetətɪv/ *adj.* 竞争的

competitive advantage	比较优势
competitive positioning	竞争定位
competitive ratio	竞争比
competitive pressure	竞争压力
competitive nature	竞争本能

Much research has been conducted into the relation between competitive strategy and firm performance.
已有许多研究考察了竞争策略和公司表现之间的关系。

Day 197

fuel

/ˈfjuːəl/ *n.* 燃料；燃烧剂

fuel moisture	可燃物含水率
fuel type	燃料类型
fuel load	燃料负荷
fuel treatment	可燃物处理
fossil **fuel**	化石燃料

The three cost change parameters reflect the first unit cost of a renewable resource compared to electricity derived from fossil fuels.
三个成本变化的参数反映了可再生资源的第一个单位成本，与从化石燃料中获取的电力进行比较。

agile

/ˈædʒaɪl/ *adj.* 敏捷的

agile method	敏捷方法
agile software	敏捷软件
agile development	敏捷开发

However, agile methodologies alone would not work in every case.
然而,敏捷方法本身并不适用于每一种情况。

Day 198

flux

/flʌks/ *n.* (物理)通量,能流;辐射(或粒子)通量;电通量

numerical flux	数值通量
energy flux	能量通量
sediment flux	泥沙流通量;沉积物通量
flux reconstruction	通量重建
flux equilibrium	通量平衡

Numerical flux is used to evaluate the integrand in line integrals.
数值通量用于评估线积分中的被积函数。

abstract

/ˈæbstrækt/ *adj.* 抽象的

abstract syntax	抽象句法
abstract authorization	抽象授权
abstract model	抽象模型
abstract data	抽象数据
abstract security	抽象安全

We do not compare two sets of exact values, but rather compare two abstract data models.
我们并没有比较两组确切值,而是比较了两组抽象数据模型。

Day 199

paradigm

/ˈpærədaɪm/ *n.* 范式；样板

classical **paradigm**	古典范式
visual **paradigm**	视觉范式
interaction **paradigm**	交互范式
research **paradigm**	研究范式
dominant **paradigm**	主导范式

The Web has become the dominant paradigm for electronic access to information services.
对于信息服务，网络已成为主导范式。

fraction

/ˈfrækʃn/ *n.* 分数；小数；小部分

fraction problem	分数问题
fraction method	分数法
fraction weighting	分数加权
fraction refinement	分数细化
volume **fraction**	体积分数

We should pay attention to the fraction weighting.
我们应当留意分数加权。

Day 200

taxonomy

/tækˈsɒnəmi/ *n.* 分类学；分类法

reference **taxonomy**	参考分类
prototype **taxonomy**	原型分类
tree-like **taxonomy**	树状分类法

In addition, it presents a practical taxonomy for collecting, managing, and using the reference architecture effectively.
此外,本文还提出了一个实践性的分类方法,用以有效地收集、管理和使用参考体系结构。

exceed

/ɪkˈsiːd/ *v.* 超出;超过

exceed the threshold	超过阈值
exceed the number	超过数字
exceed the range	超过区间
exceed the density	超过密度

Large networks cannot be displayed as the number of nodes may exceed the number of pixels.
大型网络可能无法展示,因为节点数量可能超过像素数量。

第三部分
三星词汇

Day 201

enforce
/ɪnˈfɔːs/ v. 实施；执行

enforce the policy	实施政策
enforce the updating	实施更新
enforce the service	实施服务
enforce the decision	实施决定

We propose an algorithm to enforce the policy while reducing the risk exposure of the system.
我们提出了一种算法实施政策，降低系统暴露的风险。

efficiently
/ɪˈfɪʃntli/ adv. 高效地

work efficiently	高效地工作
solve the problem efficiently	高效解决问题
perform the task efficiently	高效完成任务
compute efficiently	高效计算

We also maintain that other architectures that use similar structures could also work efficiently.
我们同样认为，其他有着相似结构的构架同样效率很高。

Day 202

couple
/ˈkʌpl/ v. 加上；结合

couple with other tools	与其他工具一起
couple with each other	彼此结合在一起

These two courses act in the same direction and therefore couple with each other positively.
这两个进程方向相同，因此彼此可以积极推进。

infer

/ɪnˈfɜː(r)/ v. 推断；推论

infer the parameters	推断参数
infer the classification	推断分类
infer the answer	推断答案
infer the activities	推断活动

Therefore, the aim is to infer the parameters of an appliance type.
因此，目的是通过设备类型推断参数。

Day 203

violate

/ˈvaɪəleɪt/ v. 违反；违背；侵犯

violate rules	违反规则
violate policies	违反政策
violate standards	违反标准
violate norms	违反规范

These results give further evidence that neutralization is an important predictor of the intentions to violate security policies.
这些结果进一步证明中和作用是违反安全政策的重要预测。

abstraction

/æbˈstrækʃn/ n. 抽象；提取；抽象概念

programming abstraction	编程抽象
network abstraction	网络抽象
model abstraction	抽象模型
design abstraction	抽象设计

The focus of this work is different in that it addresses programming abstractions to facilitate implementations of in-network data estimation algorithms.
这部著作的焦点有所不同，它采用抽象程序促进网络内数据估计算法的实施。

Day 204

digital
/ˈdɪdʒɪtl/ *adj.* 数字的

digital forensics	数字取证
digital signature	数字签名
digital certificate	数字证书
digital media	数字媒体
digital preservation	数字化保藏；数位保存

Digital libraries are not well-suited to complex automated searches.
数字图书馆并不适用于复杂的自动检索。

hardware
/ˈhɑːdweə(r)/ *n.* 计算机硬件

hardware configuration	硬件配置表
hardware device	硬件部件
hardware platform	硬件平台
hardware module	硬件模块
hardware technology	硬件技术

The hardware device itself was criticised as being inconvenient to carry around.
人们批评硬件设备本身不易携带。

Day 205

schema
/ˈskiːmə/ *n.* 纲要；图解

database schema	数据库模式
XML schema	可延伸标示语言概要；可扩展标记语言模式
conceptual schema	概率模式；概念框图

schema evolution	模式演化
schema matching	模式匹配

Database schema needs to evolve in order to adapt to requirement changes and to facilitate the maintenance of databases.
数据库模式需要演进以适应不断变化的需求，促进数据库的维护。

character

/ˈkærəktə(r)/ *n.* 字符；最小信息记录单元；特征

network character	网络特征
neighboring character	相邻字符
physical character	物理特性
performance character	性能特征
common character	常见字符

The construction of the R-table is performed to record all spatial description of neighboring character pairs of each model.
我们构建了一个R表格来记录每个模型相邻字符的所有空间描述。

Day 206

logical

/ˈlɒdʒɪkl/ *adj.* 逻辑的

logical model	逻辑模型
logical system	逻辑体系
logical approach	逻辑方法
logical framework	逻辑框架
logical theory	逻辑理论

The domain ontology may be represented using any logical model.
领域本体可以借助任何逻辑模型展示。

implicit

/ɪmˈplɪsɪt/ *adj.* 含蓄的；未言明的

implicit authentication	隐式身份验证
implicit information	内含信息
implicit feedback	隐式反馈
implicit knowledge	内隐知识
implicit code	隐式代码

Literal values are linked to code list items for various kinds of dimensions and code lists, and implicit code lists are extracted from the data.
字面值与隐式代码和代码列表在各种各样的维度相连,隐式代码列表从数据中提取。

Day 207

optimize

/ˈɒptɪmaɪz/ *v.* 优化;充分利用

optimize the value	充分利用值
optimize the parameters	充分利用参数
optimize the data	充分利用数据
optimize the transformation	充分利用转换
optimize the digitization	优化数字化

It is therefore desirable to optimize the performance measure.
因此,最理想的方式是优化绩效衡量。

discovery

/dɪˈskʌvəri/ *n.* 发现;发现的事物

information **discovery**	信息披露
knowledge **discovery**	知识发现
resource **discovery**	资源发现
cluster **discovery**	聚类模式挖掘
data **discovery**	数据发现

Performance of queries and search mechanisms for data discovery can be significantly improved when syntactic and semantic heterogeneity among datasets is overcome.
如果我们克服了数据集中句法和语义的异质性,那么数据发现中的检索和搜索机制就可以得到很大改善。

Day 208

quantify

/ˈkwɒntɪfaɪ/ *v.* 测定……的数量；量化

quantify the performance	量化表现
quantify the sensitivity	量化灵敏度
quantify the influence	量化影响
quantify the benefits	量化益处
quantify the efficiency	量化效率

As our main contribution, we develop and quantify the performance of a number of reductive methods.
我们的主要贡献是设计和量化了一系列还原方法的表现。

repository

/rɪˈpɒzətri/ *n.* （计算机）数据库

data **repository**	数据库
central **repository**	中央仓库
online **repository**	在线代码仓库
learning **repository**	学习存储库
software **repository**	软件存储库

We also recorded them in our online data repository whenever we noticed such reported data.
只要我们注意到这样的报告数据，就会把它们记录到线上数据存储库中。

Day 209

identifier

/aɪˈdentɪfaɪə(r)/ *n.* 识别符

resource **identifier**	资源识别符
source **identifier**	源识别符
fragment **identifier**	片段识别符

entity **identifier**	实体识别符
common **identifier**	常见识别符

Resources in the "ns" class are allowed to use fragment identifiers.
"ns"类中的资源允许使用片段识别符。

manually

/ˈmænjuəli/ *adv.* 手动地

manually annotated	手动标注
manually identified	手动识别
manually selected	手动选择
manually classify	手动分类
manually assess	手动评价

Section 4 reports the experimental results compared to manually identified principal lines.
第四节比较了实验结果和手动识别主线的不同。

Day 210

exhibit

/ɪɡˈzɪbɪt/ *v.* 展示;展出

exhibit the same sensitivity	展示出相同的敏感度
exhibit the advantages	展示出优势
exhibit the disadvantages	展示出劣势
exhibit the characteristics	展示出特征

Not surprisingly, the questions do not exhibit the same degree of correlation.
意料之中的是,这些问题并没有展示出相同程度的相关性。

mathematical

/ˌmæθəˈmætɪkl/ *adj.* 数学的

mathematical model	数学模型
mathematical programming	数学规划
mathematical formulation	数学公式

| **mathematical** basis | 数学基础 |
| **mathematical** description | 数学描述 |

Our mathematical model uses fuzzy cognitive maps.
我们的数学模型使用了模糊认知图。

Day 211

schedule

/ˈʃedjuːl/ *n.* 计划表;表单

project **schedule**	项目进度表
communication **schedule**	通信调度;通信时程
run-time **schedule**	运行时安排

In summary, the most likely scenario for these projects is that poor project schedule estimates are based on inadequate requirements information.
总之,对于这些项目来说,不良项目计划预期最可能的情形是需求信息不足。

conditional

/kənˈdɪʃənl/ *adj.* 有条件的;有前提的

conditional probability	条件概率
conditional independence	条件独立性
conditional entropy	条件熵
conditional pattern	条件模式
conditional distribution	条件分布

Note that the conditional distribution is part of the definition.
请注意条件分布正是定义的一部分。

Day 212

buffer

/ˈbʌfə(r)/ *n.* 存储;缓存数据

distance **buffer**	缓冲距离
buffer threshold	缓冲阈值
buffer overflow	缓冲区溢出
buffer size	缓冲区大小
buffer level	缓冲水平

We are also interested in the maximum buffer size at coding points.
我们同样对编码区连接的最大缓冲区感兴趣。

trace

/treɪs/ *n.* 跟踪；追踪

numerical **trace**	数值追踪
execution **trace**	执行追踪
matrix **trace**	矩阵的迹
synthetic **trace**	合成描线
normal **trace**	正常轨迹

The choice of numerical traces determines the results.
数值追踪的选择决定了结果。

Day 213

automatic

/ˌɔːtəˈmætɪk/ *adj.* 自动的；必然的

automatic test	自动测试
automatic generation	自动生成
automatic cluster	自动聚类
automatic annotation	自动标注
automatic approach	自动方法

The work in this paper attempts to combine two research areas through an automatic testing framework.
本论文尝试借助一个自动测试框架将两个研究领域整合起来。

normalize

/ˈnɔːməlaɪz/ v. 正常化,标准化;使用标准格式表示

normalize the scores	成绩标准化
normalize the input	输入标准化
normalize the function	功能标准化
normalize the cost	成本标准化
normalize the elements	元素标准化

We normalize the scores before performing the fusion.
我们在融合之前实现了成绩标准化。

Day 214

collaboration

/kəˌlæbəˈreɪʃn/ n. 合作;协作

distributed **collaboration**	分布式协作
active **collaboration**	积极合作
scientific **collaboration**	科学合作
multi-agency **collaboration**	多部门协作
face-to-face **collaboration**	面对面合作

Geographically distributed collaboration has long been an important topic of study.
地理分布式协作一直是研究中的重要课题。

approximate

/əˈprɒksɪmət/ v. 模仿,模拟;粗略估计

approximate the optimal number	模拟最大数值
approximate the solution	模拟解决方案
approximate the velocity	模拟速度
approximate the trajectory	模拟轨迹
approximate the weight	模拟权重

Our mathematical model uses fuzzy cognitive maps.
我们的数学模型使用了模糊认知图。

Day 215

intermediate

/ˌɪntəˈmiːdiət/ *adj.* 居中的;中等程度的

intermediate node	中间节点
intermediate results	中间结果
intermediate velocity	中间速度
intermediate vertex	中间顶点

The data includes both simulation end results and intermediate data files generated prior to and during the simulation process.
数据包括模拟过程之前和中间的仿真最终结果和中间数据文档。

adoption

/əˈdɒpʃn/ *n.* 采纳;采用

widespread adoption	广泛采用
technology adoption	技术采纳
market adoption	市场应用
software adoption	软件采用
initial adoption	初期采用

In the past, technology adoption studies have focused mainly on behavioral intent without actually measuring initial use.
过去,技术采纳研究主要关注行为目的,而没有衡量最初用途。

Day 216

formulate

/ˈfɔːmjuleɪt/ *v.* 制定,规划;提出

formulate the optimization problem	制定优化问题
formulate the variable precision	制定可变精度

| formulate the resource allocation | 提出资源分配问题 |
| formulate the network | 制定网络 |

We formulated the resource allocation problem.
我们提出了资源分配问题。

feasible

/ˈfiːzəbl/ *adj.* 可行的

feasible solution	可行解决方案
feasible schedule	可行计划
feasible parameter	可行参数
feasible distance	可行距离
feasible reasoning	可行推理

The resource provisioning objective is to find a feasible solution minimizing the total required bandwidth to be reserved on the set of edges.
资源供应的目标是找到可行解决方案最大限度降低边集中的总带宽。

Day 217

hidden

/ˈhɪdn/ *adj.* 隐藏的;隐秘的

hidden layer	隐藏层
hidden node	隐藏节点
hidden information	隐藏信息
hidden variable	隐变数;隐变量

We also hypothesize that another hidden variable is a state variable.
我们同时假设另一个隐藏变量是一个状态变量。

latency

/ˈleɪtənsi/ *n.* 所需时间;时延

access **latency**	访问等待时间
network **latency**	网络传输延迟时间
ring **latency**	环形等待时间（延迟）
detection **latency**	检测延迟
path **latency**	路径延迟

Therefore, the network latency seems to be a factor limiting the scalability in our experimental setting.
因此，网络传输延迟时间似乎限制了试验设置中的可扩展性。

Day 218

adaptation

/ˌædæpˈteɪʃn/ *n.* 调试；适应

dynamic **adaptation**	动态适应
fine-grained **adaptation**	细颗粒度适应
modular **adaptation**	模块化适应
software **adaptation**	软件适应

We apply our adaptation approach to cell biology simulations.
我们采用适应方法进行细胞生物模拟。

quantity

/ˈkwɒntəti/ *n.* 数量；数目

threshold **quantity**	临界量
vector **quantity**	矢量，向量
user-definable **quantity**	用户自行设定的数量
quantity space	数量空间
quantity test	数量测试

In our model, influences were exerted continuously and were cumulative, causing changes only when a threshold quantity was received.
我们模型中的影响是持续的、累加的，只有阈值量发生变化时才会改变。

Day 219

transfer
/trænsˈfɜː(r)/ n. 传递；转移；转换

knowledge **transfer**	知识传递
message **transfer**	信息传递
heat **transfer**	热传递
network **transfer**	网络传递

In addition, for both the sequential and dependent distribution patterns, daily knowledge transfer between sites is needed.
除此之外，对于顺序和依存分布模式来讲，网站之间每日知识传递是必要的。

classical
/ˈklæsɪkl/ adj. 经典的；传统的

classical paradigm	经典范式
classical planning	经典规划
classical approach	经典方法
classical problem	经典问题
classical shape	经典形状

The classical paradigm directly matches this important characteristic of the Semantic Web.
这一经典范式直接匹配这一语义网的重要特征。

Day 220

phenomenon
/fəˈnɒmɪnən/ n. 现象

critical **phenomenon**	临界现象
similar **phenomenon**	相似现象
socio-technical **phenomenon**	社会技术现象
single **phenomenon**	单一现象

However, that a similar phenomenon was also witnessed for the VB algorithms.
然而,我们同样在 VB 算法中观察到了相似的现象。

dependency

/dɪˈpendənsi/ *n.* 从属物;依存关系

path **dependency**	路径依存
functional **dependency**	功能依存
data **dependency**	数据相关性;数据依赖性
time **dependency**	时间依存性
strong **dependency**	强依赖

Additionally, this example will be studied in the next section when the path dependency is discussed.
此外,这个例子也会在下一节的路径依存中讨论。

Day 221

remote

/rɪˈməʊt/ *adj.* 远程的

remote sensing	遥感
remote user	远程用户
remote access	远程访问
remote data	远程数据
remote surveillance	远程监控

On the other hand, remote sensing data are capable of providing synoptic views.
另一方面,遥感数据可以提供概要图像。

frequent

/ˈfriːkwənt/ *adj.* 频繁的;经常性的

frequent pattern	经常出现的模式
frequent change	经常出现的变化
frequent structure	经常出现的结构
frequent entity	经常出现的实体

As a result, no frequent pattern can be mined in this step since the frequency of both paths is less than 3.
由于两条路径的频率都低于 3，这一阶段我们无法挖掘到经常出现的模式。

Day 222

core
/kɔː(r)/ *adj.* 核心的；最重要的

core data	核心数据
core component	核心组件
core network	核心网络
core value	核心值
core function	核心功能

In step two we extend the result of step one to the core network.
在第二步中，我们把第一步的结果连接到了核心网络。

syntax
/ˈsɪntæks/ *n.* 句法；语法

abstract syntax	抽象语法
query syntax	查询语法
logic syntax	逻辑语法

Query syntax can be saved and modified subsequently such that new users get the chance to learn more expressive queries used by other researchers.
我们可以保存和修订检索语法以便新用户能够有机会学习其他研究员使用的查询表达式。

Day 223

applicable
/əˈplɪkəbl/ *adj.* 适用的；适当的

| applicable strategies | 适用策略 |
| applicable standard | 适用标准 |

applicable software	适用软件
applicable security	适用安全
applicable rule	适用规则

We identified the list of applicable software engineering topics described in Table 1.
我们从表 1 中找出了适用的软件工程话题。

transfer

/trænsˈfɜː(r)/ v. 转移；迁移

transfer the data	转移数据
transfer the file	转移文件
transfer the code	转移代码

The end-user observed delay consists of the time spent to perform tasks on one or more public clouds, and the time to transfer the data between the user's device and the clouds.
终端用户观察到的延迟包括执行一个或多个公共云任务花费的时间，以及在用户设备和云端传递数据花费的时间。

Day 224

maximum

/ˈmæksɪməm/ n. 最大值

maximum number	最大数字
maximum value	最大值
maximum likelihood	最大可能性
maximum length	最长距离
maximum level	最高水平

We wish to impose a bound on the maximum number of resources.
我们希望为资源数量最大值设定限度。

motivate

/ˈməʊtɪveɪt/ v. 成为……的原因；是……的动机

| motivate the need | 刺激需求 |
| motivate the work | 刺激工作 |

motivate the recognition	刺激识别
motivate the user	刺激用户
motivate the improvements	刺激改变

The key goal of this paper was to motivate the need for and to introduce the idea of an adaptive stabilization strategy.
本文的主要研究目标是刺激需求并引入自适应稳定策略的概念。

Day 225

default

/dɪˈfɔːlt/ n. 默认；系统设定值

default value	默认值
default parameter	默认参数
default logic	默认逻辑
default output	默认输出
default option	默认选项

The default value was used in all experiments.
默认值被用于所有实验当中。

switch

/swɪtʃ/ v. 转换；调换

switch to the new configuration	转换为新构造
switch to the policy	转换政策
switch to the appropriate variable	转换为恰当的变量

We need to decide whether or not to switch to the new value.
我们需要决定是否需要转换为新值。

Day 226

guideline

/ˈgaɪdlaɪn/ n. 指导方针；准则

implementation **guideline**	实施指南
empirical **guideline**	经验准则
general **guideline**	一般指导原则
ethical **guideline**	道德规范,道德准则
comprehensive **guideline**	全面指导

One of the major outcomes of this paper is the development of the empirical guidelines based on the synthetic tests.
本论文的一个主要成果是基于合成试验研发经验准则。

display

/dɪˈspleɪ/ *v.* 显示;展示;陈列

display the average classification accuracy	显示平均分类准确度
display the user's list	展示用户列表
display the typical behaviour	展示典型行为
display the timing	展示时间
display the results	展示结果

The figure displayed the average classification accuracy.
图片展示了平均分类准确度。

Day 227

entropy

/ˈentrəpi/ *n.* 熵(热力学函数)

conditional **entropy**	条件熵
maximum **entropy**	最大熵
approximate **entropy**	近似熵
information **entropy**	信息熵
entropy value	熵值

In order to evaluate the agreement for each relationship, we measured the information entropy of the distribution of responses.
为了评估每种关系的一致情况,我们衡量了每种回应中信息熵的分布。

project

/ˈprɒdʒekt/ v. 投影；映射

project the weighting	投射权重
project the data	展示数据
project the network	规划网络
project the features	投射特性
project the distribution	投射分布

One means of doing this is to project the data onto a low dimensional space.
其中一种方法是将数据投射到低维空间。

Day 228

convert

/kənˈvɜːt/ v. 转换；转变

convert the data into a more structured format	将数据转化为结构化形式
convert the technical and strategic dimensions into the economic dimension	将技术和策略维度转化为经济维度
convert the task into a classification problem	将任务转化为一个分类问题
convert the outcome of the algorithm	转化算法结果
convert the image	转化图像

We converted the data into a more structured format.
我们把数据转化为一个结构化更强的形式。

translate

/trænzˈleɪt/ v. 转换（计算机程序或语言所含的信息）；改编；改写

translate the elements	转换元素
translate the interface	转换界面
translate the annotation	转换标注
translate the essential features	转换重要特征
translate the ontology	转换本体

We translated the elements of the experience.
我们转换了体验元素。

Day 229

minimum

/ˈmɪnɪməm/ *n.* 最小值；最低限度

determine the **minimum**	决定最小值
find the **minimum**	找出最小值
estimate the **minimum**	预估最小值
compute the **minimum**	计算最小值
provide the **minimum**	提供最小值

We can exactly compute the minimum.
我们可以准确计算最小值。

stochastic

/stɒˈkæstɪk/ *adj.* 随机的；猜测的

stochastic simulation	随机模拟
stochastic optimization	随机优化
stochastic dominance	随机优势
stochastic search	随机搜寻
stochastic method	随机方法

Even though recent advanced stochastic optimization algorithms (see Section 3) can efficiently address the first two aforementioned problems.
即使是近期先进的随机优化算法（详见第三节），都可以有效处理前面提到的两个问题。

Day 230

allocate

/ˈæləkeɪt/ *v.* 分配；划拨

allocate the work	分配工作
allocate the virtual server	分配虚拟服务器
allocate the tag	分配标签
allocate the radiograph	分配射线照片
allocate the external behaviour	分配外部行为

The current prototype lacks the logic required to safely allocate the work.
目前的原型缺乏安全分配工作的逻辑。

overlap

/ˌəʊvəˈlæp/ v. 与……重叠

overlap with the path	与路径重叠
overlap with the value	与值重叠
overlap with the test	与测试重叠
overlap with each other	彼此相互重叠
overlap with the other neighboring cells	与邻近细胞重叠

Previous robotic systems have typically assumed that word concepts can overlap with each other.
此前机器人系统尝尝假设词概念可以相互重叠。

Day 231

card

/kɑːd/ n. 卡片

sound **card**	声卡
smart **card**	智能卡
graphics **card**	显卡
security **card**	安全卡
payment **card**	支付卡

The location of the nodes and edges are copied onto the graphics card.
我们将节点和临界点的位置拷贝到了显卡当中。

bit

/bɪt/ n. 位

32 **bit**	32位
flag **bit**	标志位
binary **bit**	二进位；[数]二进制位
constant **bit** rate	恒定比特率、固定位元率
alternating **bit** protocol	交替位协议

As an explanatory case study, we present the alternating bit protocol.
作为探索性案例研究,我们展示了交替位协议。

Day 232

iterative
/ˈɪtərətɪv/ *adj.* 迭代的

iterative solution	迭代解
iterative process	迭代过程
iterative approach	迭代接近法
iterative development	迭代式开发
iterative algorithm	迭代算法

In this section we describe our proposed distributed iterative solution to the problem described in Section 2.
本节中我们为第二节中提出的问题提供了分布式迭代解决方案。

transmit
/trænzˈmɪt/ *v.* 传导；传输；传递

transmit data	传输数据
transmit information	传输信息
transmit value	传输值
transmit time	传输时间
transmit signal	传输信号

During execution, producer operators transmit data to consumer operators in terms of relations.
在执行阶段,生产运营商根据关系向消费运营商传输数据。

Day 233

check
/tʃek/ *n.* 校验；核查

run-time **check**	运行时检查
passport **check**	护照检查
integrity **check**	完整性检查
function **check**	功能检查
signature **check**	签名检查

The essential computation applied in symbolic model checking is efficient.
符号模型检测的重要计算十分有效。

weighted
/ˈweɪtɪd/ *adj.* 加权的；加重的

weighted sum	加权和
weighted average	加权平均
weighted mean difference	加权平均数差
weighted manipulation	加权处理
weighted combination	加权组合

The corresponding in-network policy computes the weighted average and variance.
对应网络政策计算加权平均数和加权方差。

Day 234

content
/ˈkɒntent/ *adj.* 内容的

content analysis	内容分析
content delivery	内容传递
content descriptor	内容描述符

content uniformity	内容一致性
content negotiation	内容协商

A content analysis was performed on the discussions of each session.
我们对每一节的内容进行了讨论分析。

realistic

/ˌriːəˈlɪstɪk/ *adj.* 务实的；实际的，现实可行的

realistic network	实际网络
realistic model	实际模型
realistic scenario	实际情形
realistic representation	实际表征
realistic simulation	实际模拟

Our preliminary numerical results are encouraging. We are able to solve a realistic model within a few seconds.
我们的最初结果十分激动人心，我们可以在几秒钟内解决一个实际模型。

Day 235

connectivity

/kəˌnekˈtɪvəti/ *n.* 连通(性)；联结(度)

network connectivity	网络连接性
Internet connectivity	互联网连接
full connectivity	全连通性
landscape connectivity	景观连接度
database connectivity	数据库连接

Another area for future research is the network connectivity.
未来研究中的另一个研究领域是网络连接性。

yield

/jiːld/ *n.* 产量；收益

yield line	塑性铰线；屈服线
yield model	良率模式；产量模型；收获模型

We compared the performance of an empirical forest growth and yield model and a gap model.
我们比较了实证森林增长、产量模型和间隔模型的表现差异。

Day 236

operational

/ˌɒpəˈreɪʃənl/ *adj.* 正常运转的；操作的，运营的

operational state	作业状态
operational definitions	操作性定义
operational performance	运营绩效
operational environment	操作环境
operational research	运筹学

Internal and external changes to the operational environment such as service channel expansions and the current economic climate will therefore have a significant impact upon account usage.
操作环境的内部和外部变化，例如业务渠道拓展和当前经济环境都会对账户使用产生重要影响。

delete

/dɪˈliːt/ *v.* 删除

delete the file	删除文档
delete the project	删除项目
delete the link	删除链接
delete the annotation	删除标注
delete the command	删除命令

Additionally, learners may add or delete data at any time.
此外，学习者可以在任何时间添加或删除数据。

Day 237

computationally
/kɒm.pjəˈteɪʃənəli/ *adv.* 运算地

computationally efficient quick sort algorithm	运算高效的快速分类算法
the most **computationally** expensive component	运算成本最高的算法
computationally infeasible	运算上无法实现
computationally expensive black-box optimization	运算成本较高的黑盒优化

Resolving the solution on the fine scale is often computationally infeasible.
我们无法在细小刻度上解决运算问题。

translation
/trænzˈleɪʃn/ *n.* 转移；平移；转化；翻译

machine **translation**	机器翻译
automatic **translation**	自动翻译
translation process	翻译过程
translation algorithm	翻译算法
translation invariant	平移不变性

However, the results from the first experiment provided us insight to improve the translation process.
然而，第一个实验的结果为我们改善翻译过程提供了启示。

Day 238

diffusion
/dɪˈfjuːʒn/ *n.* 扩散；传播

knowledge **diffusion**	知识扩散
reverse **diffusion**	逆行扩散
information **diffusion**	信息扩散
numerical **diffusion**	数值扩散
chemical **diffusion**	化学扩散

We investigate the importance of active communicators in knowledge diffusion.
我们调查了主动传播者在知识传播中的重要性。

portion

/ˈpɔːʃn/ *n.* 某物中的一份；一部分

a **portion**	一部分
a large **portion**	一大部分
a small **portion**	一小部分
a significant **portion**	很大一部分

This will cause a noticeable slowdown for a significant portion of the Internet.
这会使网络中很大一部分速度显著下降。

Day 239

displacement

/dɪsˈpleɪsmənt/ *n.* 电位移

nonlinear **displacement**	非线性位移
maximum **displacement**	最大位移
horizontal **displacement**	水平位移
vertical **displacement**	垂直位移
linear **displacement**	线性位移

Fig. 25 and Fig. 26 show comparisons for the time history of the horizontal displacements.
图 25 和图 26 比较了水平位移的时间历史。

recovery

/rɪˈkʌvəri/ *n.* 恢复

architecture **recovery**	构架恢复
design **recovery**	设计恢复
route **recovery**	路线恢复
material **recovery**	资料回收
energy **recovery**	能量恢复

Architecture recovery tools are essential for diagnosing architectural problems.
构架恢复工具对诊断构架问题至关重要。

Day 240

count

/kaʊnt/ *n.* 计数

loop **count**	循环计数
multiple **count**	多重计数
element **count**	数据单元计数；元素计数
algebraic **count**	代数计算

In many cases, a loop count variable needs to be created.
很多情况下,我们需要创造一个循环计数变量。

maximize

/ˈmæksɪmaɪz/ *v.* 最大限度；把……最大化

maximize the utility	效用最大化
maximize the probability	概率最大化
maximize the average	均值最大化
maximize the representativeness	代表性最大化
maximize the likelihood	可能性最大化

We updated the parameters in order to maximize the likelihood.
我们更新了参数,以便使可能性最大化。

Day 241

enterprise

/ˈentəpraɪz/ *n.* 企业

enterprise server	企业服务器
enterprise security	企业安全

enterprise system	企业系统
enterprise resource	企业资源
enterprise software	企业软件

Variants on these exemplar methodologies have been adopted into enterprise security policies and standards.
范例方法变体已经为企业安全策略和标准采纳。

fusion

/ˈfjuːʒn/ n. 融合；结合

feature fusion	特征融合
loop fusion	循环合并；回圈融合
data fusion	数据融合
hybrid fusion	混合融合
information fusion	信息融合

We used a variety of applications including expert systems, information fusion, risk analysis and artificial intelligence.
我们使用了各式各样的应用，包括专家系统、信息融合、危险分析和人工智能。

Day 242

histogram

/ˈhɪstəɡræm/ n. 直方图；柱状图

velocity histogram	速度直方图
distance histogram	距离直方图
color histogram	颜色直方图
normalized histogram	规格化直方图

Fig. 5 illustrates the characteristic changes that the velocity histogram.
图 5 展示了速度直方图的特征变化。

propagate

/ˈprɒpəɡeɪt/ v. 传播（运动、光线、声音等）

propagate information	传播信息
propagate the solution	传播解决方案

The back propagation set is used to propagate information.
反向传播组用于传播信息。

Day 243

respective
/rɪˈspektɪv/ *adj.* 分别的；各自的

respective organisation	相关机构
respective spectrograms	各自的光谱图
respective sample	相关样本
respective parameter	相应参数

We compared the algorithm with their respective parameters.
我们对比了算法和相应参数。

collaborative
/kəˈlæbərətɪv/ *adj.* 合作的；协作的

collaborative intrusion	协同入侵
collaborative systems	协同系统
collaborative authentication	协同验证
collaborative work	协同工作
collaborative development	协同发展

The holistic and collaborative development process and the design artifacts are outlined in Section 5.
整体和协同发展过程以及设计产物位于第五节中。

Day 244

trigger
/ˈtrɪɡə(r)/ *v.* 引发；刺激

trigger the evolution	引发进化
trigger the creation	引发创造

trigger the application of methods	引发方法应用
trigger the automatic execution	引发自动运行

For both types of access the information required to trigger the transition may be distributed across several objects.
两种获取信息引发转变的方式可能分布在不同物体当中。

gradient

/ˈɡreɪdiənt/ *n.* (温度或压力变化的)梯度;(数学)斜率;梯度,梯度率

gradient descent	梯度下降
gradient vector	梯度向量
gradient variation	梯度变化
gradient information	梯度信息
gradient magnitude	梯度幅值

The gradient vector would be going perpendicular to the level.
梯度向量应该垂直于等值线。

Day 245

correspondence

/ˌkɒrəˈspɒndəns/ *n.* 通信;对应

point **correspondence**	点对应
one-to-one **correspondence**	一一对应
concept **correspondence**	概念对应
semantic **correspondence**	语义对应

We attempt to find semantic correspondences between varying terminologies.
我们尝试找出不同术语之间的语义对应关系。

independently

/ˌɪndɪˈpendəntli/ *adv.* 独立地

developed **independently**	独立开发
used **independently**	独立使用
processed **independently**	独立处理

solved **independently**	独立解决
executed **independently**	独立执行

A complex problem is decomposed into several sub-problems that are solved independently.
一个复杂问题被分解为多个可以独立解决的子问题。

Day 246

accurately

/ˈækjərətli/ *adv.* 精确地；准确地

measured **accurately**	准确测量
analysed **accurately**	准确分析
understood **accurately**	准确理解
tracked **accurately**	准确追踪

We assumed that the orientation attribute is measured accurately.
我们假设定位属性得到了准确测量。

constrain

/kənˈstreɪn/ *v.* 限制；约束；迫使

constrain the shape	限制形状
constrain the search	限制搜索
constrain the use	限制使用
constrain the number	限制数字
constrain the motion	限制移动

We constrain the number of components to be the same for all the mixture models.
我们限制了混合模型成分数量，使其做到一致。

Day 247

synthetic

/sɪnˈθetɪk/ *adj.* 合成的；人造的；综合的

synthetic dimensions	合成维度
synthetic networks	合成网络
synthetic datasets	合成数据集
synthetic sequences	合成序列
synthetic model	合成模型

These results suggest that, in the synthetic networks considered, social and environmental factors are of similar importance.
这些结果表明,在合成网络中,社会和环境因素同样重要。

sequential

/sɪˈkwenʃl/ *adj.* 连续的;相继发生的

sequential decision	序贯判定
sequential inference	顺序推理
sequential information	连续信息
sequential data	顺序数据
sequential classification	顺序分类

For climate mitigation, this equates to a sequential decision-making strategy.
对于气候缓解,这相当于序列决策策略。

Day 248

matching

/ˈmætʃɪŋ/ *n.* 匹配

pattern matching	模式匹配
maximum matching	最大匹配,最大配对
shape matching	形状匹配
structural matching	结构匹配
string matching	字符串匹配

In summary, these algorithms focus on space and time efficiency of the pattern matching.
总之,这些算法聚焦空间和时间效率的模式匹配。

structured

/ˈstrʌktʃəd/ *adj.* 有结构的;有组织的

structured interview	结构化面试
structured data	结构化数据
structured pattern	结构化模式
structured knowledge	结构化知识
structured grid	结构网络,结构性网络

The essential difference between the classic Web and the Semantic Web is that structured data is exposed in a structured way.
经典网络和语义网络的重要差别是结构化数据的呈现方式。

Day 249

coarse

/kɔːs/ *adj.* 粗糙的;粗鲁的

coarse granularity	粗粒度
coarse representation	粗表征
coarse model	粗糙模型
coarse interfaces	粗糙界面

The function codes shall implement the first stage coarse granularity security selector shown in Fig. 4.
功能代码将实现图 4 中第一阶段粗粒度安全选择。

polygon

/ˈpɒlɪɡən/ *n.* 多边形;多角形物体

polygon space	多边形空间
polygon detector	多边形探测器
polygon detection	多边形检测
polygon transform	多边形转换
polygon size	多边形大小

It creates spatial correlation and a larger average polygon size.
它创造了空间关系和一个更大的平均多边形。

Day 250

formally
/ˈfɔːməli/ *adv.* 正式地；传统地

formally defined	正式定义
formally described	正式描述
formally introduce	正式介绍
formally understood	正式理解

As formally defined in the preceding section, IANA is the root node.
正如前一节正式定义的那样，IANA 是根节点。

prepossessing
/ˌpriːpəˈzesɪŋ/ *n.* 预处理

preprocessing technique	预处理技术
preprocessing stage	预处理阶段
preprocessing mismatch	预处理不匹配
preprocessing information	预处理信息
preprocessing method	预处理方法

None of the previous studies have listed or compared the data preprocessing techniques.
此前从未有研究列出并比较了预处理技术。

Day 251

target
/ˈtɑːɡɪt/ *v.* 把……作为对象，把……作为目标

target the problem of exploiting the environmental variable	聚焦挖掘环境变量的问题
target the specific problem	聚焦特定问题
target the forecast	聚焦预测

The low-level aspects target the problems of exploiting the environmental variables.
低水平层面主要聚集探索环境变量的问题。

compromise

/ˈkɒmprəmaɪz/ *v.* 妥协；折中

compromise the privacy of data	在数据隐私上妥协
compromise the network	在网络上妥协

This method does not compromise the privacy of data.
这一方法并没有在数据隐私上妥协。

Day 252

setup

/ˈsetʌp/ *n.* （软件或硬件的）安装；设置

experimental **setup**	实验设置
system **setup**	系统设置
simulation **setup**	模拟设置
evaluation **setup**	评价设置
connection **setup**	连接设置

Section 4 describes approaches for user-oriented evaluation, such as the experimental setup and criteria to be assessed.
第四节描述了以用户为导向的评价方法，例如实验设置和需要评价的标准。

span

/spæn/ *v.* 持续；贯穿；横跨

span the whole graph	横跨整幅图片
span the entire product lifecycle	贯穿整个产品生命周期
span the space	贯穿整个空间
span the problem	贯穿问题
span the solution	贯穿解决方案

The e-hub now serves 2700 partners by supporting an electronic connection and training service for activities that span the entire product lifecycle.

数字中枢现在服务着 2700 位合作伙伴，支持电子连接，为整个产品生命周期的活动提供培训服务。

Day 253

visualization

/ˌvɪʒuəlaɪˈzeɪʃn/ *n.* 形象化；视觉化

data **visualization**	数据可视化
network **visualization**	网络可视化
information **visualization**	信息可视化
dynamic **visualization**	动态可视化
map **visualization**	地图可视化

Dimensionality reduction is an important step in pattern recognition, classification and data visualization.
降维是模式识别、分类和数据可视化中的重要一步。

modified

/ˈmɒdɪfaɪd/ *adj.* 改进的；修改的；改良的

modified version	经过修改的版本
modified method	经过修改的方法
modified algorithm	经过修正的算法
modified goal	经过修正的目标

We used the data sets from Table 2 to verify the performance of the modified algorithms.
我们使用了表 2 的数据集验证经过修订的算法。

Day 254

generator

/ˈdʒenəreɪtə(r)/ *n.* 发电机；产生者；电力公司

number **generator**	[电子]数字发生器;[电子]数码发生器
test **generator**	[计]测试生成程序
data **generator**	数据发生器
topology **generator**	拓扑生成器
graph **generator**	图形发生器

We used a random number generator to find a value within the given range.
我们使用了一个随机数生成器找出给定区间的值。

simultaneously

/ˌsɪmlˈteɪnɪəsli/ *adv.* 同时地

simultaneously segment	同时分割
simultaneously take	同时采用
simultaneously sample	同时取样
simultaneously reduce	同时减少
simultaneously minimize	同时把……降到最低

This is a powerful way of selecting the optimal features that simultaneously minimizes both the lower and upper bound.
这是一个强有力的方式,选取最优特征,同时最大限度降低上限和下限。

Day 255

flexible

/ˈfleksəbl/ *adj.* 灵活的;柔韧的,易弯曲的

flexible way	灵活的方式
flexible software	柔性软件,灵活软件
flexible platform	灵活的平台
flexible framework	灵活的框架
flexible model	灵活的模型

There is a consequent need for flexible software environments for hydrological modelling.
因而就需要为水文建模准备灵活的软件环境。

electronic

/ɪˌlekˈtrɒnɪk/ *adj.* 电子的；电子学的

electronic density	电子密度
electronic commerce	电子商务
electronic trading	电子贸易
electronic health	电子健康
electronic markets	电子市场

Electronic commerce is particularly vulnerable to network related threats, such as virus infection and disruptive software.
电子商务很容易受到网络相关威胁的影响，例如病毒感染和软件破坏。

Day 256

outlier

/ˈaʊtlaɪə(r)/ *n.* (统计)异常值

outlier detection	离群点检测
outlier candidate	离群值候选
outlier value	离群值
outlier number	离群数字
outlier measurement	离群值测量

They are then used as input to a density-based outlier detection algorithm.
接下来，它们作为离群点检测算法输入。

array

/əˈreɪ/ *n.* 一系列；大量；数组；数阵

array programming	阵列编程
array problem	数组问题
array vector	数组矢量；[计]数组向量
array expression	[计]数组表达式
array variable	[计]数组变量

The required array programming entirely relies on free software.
所需阵列编程完全依赖免费软件。

Day 257

annotate
/ˈænəteɪt/ v. 注释；给……做标注

annotate resources	标注资源
annotate document	标注文档
annotate the examples	标注例子
annotate the entity	标注实体
annotate the graph	标注图表

The same production rule can successfully be applied to also annotate the results.
同样的生产式规则可以成功用于标注结果。

positive
/ˈpɒzətɪv/ adj. 正的；肯定的；积极的

positive probability	实证概率
positive approximation	正逼近
positive effect	积极影响
positive relationship	正向关系
positive rate	阳性率

In each case a strong positive relationship was indicated.
每个案例中都显示出很强的正向关系。

Day 258

predictor
/prɪˈdɪktə(r)/ n. 预测器；预示物

predictor variable	预测变量
predictor coefficient	预测系数
predictor feature	预测特征
predictor set	预测集
predictor parameter	预测参数

However, as efficiency was only related to effectiveness and not to any of the predictor variables, it was decided to conduct just one hierarchical regression.
然而,既然效率只与有效性相关,与其他任何预测变量无关,因此我们决定只进行一次层次回归。

log

/lɒg/ n. 对数;(定期或系统的)观察记录;船舶测速仪

log file	日志文件
log paradigm	日志模式
log data	日志数据
log likelihood	对数似然
log analysis	日志分析

This model was actually extracted from the query log files that collect user interactions with a library catalogue search engine.
事实上,这一模型从查询日志文件中提取,借助图书馆目录搜索引擎收集用户互动。

Day 259

compute

/kəmˈpjuːt/ n. 计算;估算

algorithm compute	算法计算
parallel compute	平行计算
performance compute	性能计算
feature compute	特征计算
statistics compute	统计计算

The first scenario assumes cloud applications use compute and cloud storage services.
第一个情形假设云应用需要计算和云存储服务器。

analytical

/ˌænəˈlɪtɪkl/ *adj.* 善于分析的;分析性的

analytical solution	解析解
analytical model	分析模型
analytical framework	分析框架
analytical formulas	分析公式
analytical expressions	解析表达式

Using the analytical solution provided above, the vapor concentration can be estimated.
使用上述分析模型,我们可以预估水汽浓度。

Day 260

composition

/ˌkɒmpəˈzɪʃn/ *n.* 成分构成

service composition	服务组合
team composition	团队构成
model composition	模型组合,模型拼装,模型复合
mapping composition	映射组成
chemical composition	化学成分

The first step introduces five models to the model composition context.
第一步是将五个模型引入模型构成的情境。

systematic

/ˌsɪstəˈmætɪk/ *adj.* 有系统的;有条理的

systematic mapping	系列制图,系列成图
systematic literature review	系统文献综述
systematic approach	系统化方法
systematic analysis	系统分析
systematic security	系统安全

A systematic literature review and knowledge synthesis approach are described using coding techniques.

我们采用编码技巧进行了系统文献综述和知识综合。

Day 261

recover

/rɪˈkʌvə(r)/ v. 恢复

recover from failures	从失败中恢复
recover from trap	从陷阱中恢复
recover from challenges	从挑战中恢复
recover information	恢复信息
recover mechanism	恢复机制

There are multiple nodes that have a complete set of indexes, so the network can recover from the failure of one node.

这里有多个包含完整索引的节点,因此网络可以从一个失败节点中恢复。

legitimate

/lɪˈdʒɪtɪmət/ adj. 正当的;合理的;合法的

legitimate users	合理用户
legitimate email	合理电子邮件
legitimate destination	合法目的地
legitimate data	合法数据
legitimate user	合法用户

The legitimate user is familiar with some or all the internal workings of the target systems.

合法用户熟悉目标系统中的部分或全部内部机制。

Day 262

detector

/dɪˈtektə(r)/ n. 探测器;检测器;发现者

tunnel detector	隧道探测器
feature detector	[生物物理]特征检测器;特征觉察器
edge detector	[测][遥感]边界检测器
hotspot detector	热点探测器
probabilistic detector	概率探测器

These feature points can be localized by either manual annotation or by an automatic feature detector.
这些特征点可以通过手动标注或自动特征探测器定位。

alignment

/əˈlaɪnmənt/ *n.* 排成直线;摆放恰当;协调,一致

semantic alignment	语义一致性
local alignment	局部比对
strategic alignment	战略对齐
optimal alignment	系统分析
sequence alignment	序列比对

A systematic literature review and knowledge synthesis approach are described using coding techniques.
我们采用编码技巧进行了系统文献综述和知识综合。

Day 263

peer

/pɪə(r)/ *n.* 等同;对等

peer network	同级网络;对等网络
peer systems	点对点系统
peer relation	同伴关系
peer project	对等项目
peer path	对等路径

Our approach is to study how we can place indexes in a peer-to-peer network to reduce system load.
本研究中的方法是研究我们如何放置对等网络索引,减轻系统载荷。

request

/rɪˈkwest/ v. (要求计算机提供信息或执行另一任务的)指令

request semantic tag	请求语义标签
request the operation	请求操作
request the data	请求数据
request the assistance	请求援助
request the input	请求输入

For instance, one application may request the semantic tags for a given document, while another may request all semantic tags regarding a particular object.

例如,一个应用可能请求特定文档的语义标签,而另一个文档可能需要某一物体的所有语义标签。

Day 264

return

/rɪˈtɜːn/ n. 返回;回车键

return period	重现期
return path	回程线路;返回路径
return address	返回地址
return search	返回搜索
return format	返回格式

The highest discharge corresponded to the current design discharge with a return period of 1250 years.

最高释放量与目前的设计流量对应,重现期为 1250 年。

versus

/ˈvɜːsəs/ prep. 与……相对;与……相比

web sites **versus** dynamic web	网站相对动态网站
each method **versus** the variation	每种方法相对差异
short term **versus** long term	短期相对长期

The second phase focused on presenting a series of business strategies and technical options for consideration of varying technical requirements and short term versus long term costs.
第二阶段关注提供一系列商业策略和技术选择，将不同技术需求和短期长期成本考虑在内。

Day 265

scalability
/ˌskeɪləˈbɪləti/ *n.* 可扩展性；可伸缩性；可量测性

scalability issue	可扩展性问题
scalability problem	可扩展性问题
scalability testing	可扩展性测试
scalability evaluation	可扩展性评估
scalability validation	可扩展性验证

Mesh networks in particular address the scalability issues of ring-based architectures.
网状网络主要处理的是环形结构的可扩展性问题。

align
/əˈlaɪn/ *v.* 使平行；调整，使一致

align very well with numerous algorithms	与许多算法十分一致
align two actions with variant time	使两个行动与变化的时间一致
align our proposal with the framework	使框架与提案一致
align our method with the risk	使方法与危险一致
align organizational structure with system structure	使组织结构与系统结构一致

The graph align very well with numerous algorithms and statistical techniques.
图表与许多算法和统计策略相一致。

Day 266

sort
/sɔːt/ *v.* 分类

sort the results	对结果进行分类
sort the node	对节点进行分类
sort the file	对文档进行分类
sort the list	对清单进行分类
sort the average value	对平均值进行分类

However, it is possible to sort the results, so that this particular problem rarely happens.
然而,由于我们可以对结果进行分类,这种问题很少发生。

snapshot

/ˈsnæpʃɒt/ n. (计算机)抽点打印;快照

experimental snapshot	实验快照
dataset snapshot	数据快照
simulation snapshot	模拟快照
snapshot technology	快照技术
snapshot version	快照版本

We adopted the snapshot technology in this experiment.
我们在此次试验中采用了快照技术。

Day 267

separately

/ˈseprətli/ adv. 单独地;分别地

treated separately	单独处理
calculated separately	单独计算
reported separately	单独报告
collected separately	单独收集
considered separately	单独考虑

Samples from each class are treated separately to consider the different distribution of the data.
考虑到数据的不同分布情况,我们单独处理每类数据样本。

endpoint

/ˈendˌpɔɪnt/ n. 端点;末端;终结点

service **endpoint**	服务端点
transfer **endpoint**	传输端点
element **endpoint**	元素端点
descriptor **endpoint**	端点描述符
default **endpoint**	默认端点

The message descriptor describes the objects that are to be used as inputs or outputs for each service endpoint.
消息描述符描述了每一个服务端点输入或输出的对象。

Day 268

video
/ˈvɪdiəʊ/ *adj.* 电视的；视频的；图像的；画面的

video search	视频搜索；影片搜寻
video sequence	视频序列
video streaming	视频流
video clip	视频剪辑
video shot	视频镜头

Global features aim to rank video clips based on their global appearances such as color, texture, shape and global spatiotemporal characters.
全局特征旨在基于视频剪辑的整体外观特征，例如颜色、材质、形状和总体时空字符对视频进行排序。

safety
/ˈseɪfti/ *n.* 安全；安全性

safety property	安全属性
safety shot	安全球
safety ratings	安全评级
safety objective	安全目标
safety network	安全网络

We cannot gather safety ratings until we know which cars for which we need ratings.
除非知道了哪些车辆需要评级，否则我们就无法收集安全评级。

Day 269

assertion
/əˈsɜːʃn/ n. 断言；明确肯定

statistical **assertion**	统计断言
property **assertion**	属性断言
histogram **assertion**	直方图断言
mapping **assertion**	映射断言
metadata **assertion**	元数据断言

Statistical assertions are useful in debugging large scale scientific problems.
统计断言对于排除大规模科学问题十分有用。

vertical
/ˈvɜːtɪkl/ adj. 垂直的；直立的

vertical axis	垂直轴
vertical structure	垂直结构
vertical cover	垂直覆盖
vertical integration	纵向整合
vertical direction	垂直方向

Fig 1 illustrates the vertical structure of the model.
图展示了模型的垂直结构。

Day 270

discharge
/dɪsˈtʃɑːdʒ/ n. 排出；释放

battery **discharge**	电池放电，蓄电池放电
peak **discharge**	洪峰流量
stormwater **discharge**	雨水排放

storm **discharge**	风暴放电
simulated **discharge**	模拟放电

There are chiefly two models of battery discharge, viz., constant current discharge and pulsed current discharge.
这里主要有两种电池放电模式,即定流放电和脉冲电流放电。

equilibrium

/ˌiːkwɪˈlɪbriəm/ *n.* 平衡;均衡

equilibrium equation	平衡方程
equilibrium climate	平衡气候
equilibrium length	平衡长度
equilibrium model	[自]均衡模型;平衡模式
equilibrium distribution	[数]平衡分布;[统计]均衡分布

The equilibrium equation is expressed at the current configuration.
我们将均衡方程展示在当前构造当中。

Day 271

corpus

/ˈkɔːpəs/ *n.* 文集;全集;语料库

training **corpus**	训练语料库
web **corpus**	网络语料库
video **corpus**	视频语料库
speech **corpus**	语音库,口语语料库
testing **corpus**	测试语料库

The emotional speech corpus was collected from this project.
这个项目收集了情感语音语料库。

battery

/ˈbætri/ *n.* 电池;蓄电池;一组;一系列

battery litter	电池垃圾
battery power	电池电量
battery life	电池寿命
battery level	电池电量
battery recycling	电池回收

There are at least 11 countries with "takeback" laws that require consumer battery recycling.
至少有 11 个国家有"回收"法,要求顾客回收电池。

Day 272

expectation
/ˌekspekˈteɪʃn/ *n.* 期望;预期

customer **expectation**	顾客期望
conditional **expectation**	条件期望
unrealistic **expectation**	不切实际的期望
subjective **expectation**	主观期望
shared **expectation**	共同期望

The study found that the top three risks were personnel shortfalls, unreasonable project schedule and budget and unrealistic expectations.
研究发现排名前三的危险因素为:人员短缺、不合理的项目规划预算和不切实际的期望。

estimator
/ˈestɪmeɪtə(r)/ *n.* [统计] 估计量;评价者

error **estimator**	误差估计
bandwidth **estimator**	带宽估计
cluster **estimator**	集群估计
quality **estimator**	质量估计
unbiased **estimator**	无偏估计量

The error estimator is based on a hierarchical approach used to control both spatial and temporal adaptivity.
误差估计基于分层方法控制空间和时间自适应性。

Day 273

rational

/ˈræʃnəl/ *adj.* 合理的;(数)有理的;有理数的

rational function	有理函数
rational cost	合理成本
rational measure	合理措施
rational choice	合理选择
rational system	合理系统

We now focus on the rational function in this study.
我们现在关注的是本研究中的有理函数。

port

/pɔːt/ *n.* 计算机端口

destination **port**	目的港口
source **port**	源端口
input **port**	输入端口
service **port**	服务端口
output **port**	输出端口

Given the fact that the attacker can easily assign arbitrary values as source ports, the source port is a highly unreliable feature.
考虑到攻击者可能轻易给任何源端口赋值,因此源端口特征十分不稳定。

Day 274

extensive

/ɪkˈstensɪv/ *adj.* 广阔的;广泛的;巨大的

| **extensive** use | 广泛使用 |
| **extensive** set | 广泛设置 |

extensive research	广泛研究
extensive experience	广泛体验
extensive review	广泛回顾

The framework proposed here makes extensive use of movable triggers.
此处提出的框架广泛使用可移动触发器。

principal

/ˈprɪnsəpl/ *adj.* 主要的；首要的；最重要的

principal components	主要成分
principal researcher	主要研究员
principal reason	主要原因
principal motivation	主要动机
principal topic	主要话题

A principal motivation for this paper is to explore the relationship between prototype theory and label semantics.
本文的主要动机是探索原型理论和标签语义学之间的关系。

Day 275

quadrature

/ˈkwɒdrətʃə/ *n.* 正交；求积；弦

quadrature rule	求积规则
quadrature points	正交工作点
quadrature weight	正交分量
quadrature scheme	正交方案
quadrature formula	[数]求积公式

They generate a quadrature rule for each cut cell by randomly choosing sampling points and computing weights.
他们通过随机选择抽样点、计算权重为每一个切割细胞生成求积规则。

meaningful

/ˈmiːnɪŋfl/ *adj.* 有意义的；重要的

meaningful overlap	有意义的重叠
meaningful way	有意义的方式
meaningful value	有意义的值
meaningful information	有意义的信息
meaningful results	有意义的结果

We detail the procedure that assigns meaningful values to the model's parameters.
我们详细描述了为模型参数赋有意义值的过程。

Day 276

block

/blɒk/ *v.* 阻塞,堵塞;阻止;拦截

block the outcome	阻止结果
block the use	阻断使用
block the transaction	阻止交易
block the request	阻止请求
block the development	阻止发展

These bugs block the development and/or testing work.
这些漏洞阻碍了发展和/或者测试作业。

fit

/fɪt/ *n.* 相配,匹配

first **fit** algorithm	最先适应法;首次适应算法

This study used the first fit algorithm.
这项研究使用了最先适应法。

Day 277

increment

/ˈɪŋkrəmənt/ *n.* (变量、函数的)正(或负)增量

volume **increment**	容积增量
simulated **increment**	模拟增量
load **increment**	载重增加；载荷增量
year-to-year **increment**	同比增加
rotation **increment**	旋转增加

For the calculation of volume increment the same method as described above in Section 2.3 was used.
为了计算容积增量，我们采用了与 3.2 小节相同的方法。

artifact

/ˈɑːtɪfækt/ *n.* 制品；构件

software **artifact**	软件构件
development **artifact**	开发构件
system **artifact**	系统构件
project **artifact**	项目构件
communication **artifact**	沟通构件

Essentially, any software artifact that can be described as a grammar can be mutated.
本质上，任何软件构件都可以描述为可以变化的语法。

Day 278

numerous

/ˈnjuːmərəs/ *adj.* 众多的；许多的

numerous studies	诸多研究
numerous data	诸多数据
numerous applications	诸多应用
numerous references	诸多参考
numerous gaps	诸多差异

Numerous studies have examined the structure of online social networks in particular, such as Blogs, Facebook and Twitter.
许多研究已经考察了线上社会网络的结构，例如博客、脸书和推特。

carrier

/ˈkæriə(r)/ *n.* 通信公司；载体

network **carrier**	网络载体
data **carrier**	［计］数据载体；数据介质；信息载体
wireless **carrier**	无线运营商
telecom **carrier**	电信运营商
mobile **carrier**	移动运营商

The mobile carrier plays a brokering role between service developers and end-users and therefore makes the decision about which service providers can create services for the portal.
移动运营商是服务开发商和终端用户的中介，因此那些服务商可以为门户网站提供服务。

Day 279

rotation

/rəʊˈteɪʃn/ *n.* 旋转；转动

object **rotation**	物体旋转
linear **rotation**	线性旋转
initial **rotation**	最初旋转
possible **rotation**	可能旋转
image **rotation**	［计］图像旋转

Most recent investigations have shown that even the routine image rotation transformation process can cause significant singular points deviation.
近期调查表明，即使是常规图像旋转变换过程也可能导致显著奇点偏差。

straightforward

/ˌstreɪtˈfɔːwəd/ *adj.* 简单的；直接的

straightforward way	直接的方式
straightforward manner	直接的方式
straightforward approach	直接的方法
straightforward calculation	简单的计算
straightforward process	简单明了的过程

The approach allows for a straightforward calculation of a probability of failure.
这种方法可以直接计算故障概率。

Day 280

manifold

/ˈmænɪfəʊld/ *n.* (数)流形；簇

linear **manifold**	[数]线性流形
dimensional **manifold**	维管汇
nonlinear **manifold**	非线性流形

Unlike conventional cluster models a linear manifold cluster is a set of points compact around a linear manifold.
与传统集群模型不同，线性流形簇是线性流形周围一系列的点。

exception

/ɪkˈsepʃn/ *n.* 例外；除外

notable **exception**	显著的例外
security **exception**	安全异常
possible **exception**	可能的例外
noteworthy **exception**	值得注意的例外
violation **exception**	违反例外

A noteworthy exception is sediment concentration measured from a single location in the cross-section.
其中一个显著例外是从跨领域单一角度衡量的沉积物浓度。

Day 281

maintenance

/ˈmeɪntənəns/ *n.* 维护；保养；保持

corrective **maintenance**	纠正性维护
ontology **maintenance**	本体维修
software **maintenance**	软件维护
security **maintenance**	安全维护

To achieve low maintenance costs, we made the model fully adaptive.
为了实现较低维护成本，我们使得模型的适应性更强。

forwarding

/ˈfɔːwədɪŋ/ *n.* 转发

packet **forwarding**	分组转发，封包转发，包转发
path **forwarding**	前进之路
greedy **forwarding**	贪婪转发
bridge **forwarding**	桥转发
multicast **forwarding**	多播转发

This location aspect has been used in the packet forwarding condition.
这一位置方面已经用于分组转发。

Day 282

insert

/ɪnˈsɜːt/ *v.* 插入；嵌入

insert card	插入卡片
insert messages	插入消息；嵌入消息
insert path	插入路径
insert operation	插入操作

The application can merge and extract messages in the knowledge set and can delete or insert messages on the communication links.
这个应用可以融合提出知识集中的信息并在通信链路上删除或插入消息。

representative

/ˌreprɪˈzentətɪv/ *adj.* 典型的；有代表性的

representative sample	代表性样本
representative set	代表性集合
representative values	代表值
representative model	代表模型
representative data	代表数据

Finally, the experimental results have been significantly extended, using a more representative data set.
最后,我们显著拓展了实验结果,采用了更具代表性的数据集。

Day 283

command

/kəˈmɑːnd/ *n.* 命令;指示;指令

control **command**	控制命令
arbitrary **command**	任意命令
padding **command**	填充命令
security **command**	安全命令
issue **command**	发布命令

This path was used subsequently and repeatedly to issue commands in the syntax.
接下来这一路径用于在句法中重复发布命令。

load

/ləʊd/ *v.* 载入(计算机程序)

load the server	载入服务器
load the task	载入任务
load the system	载入系统
load the session	载入会话
load the files	载入文档

A script was developed to request the necessary resources and load the software.
我们开发了一个脚本获取必要的资源并载入软件。

Day 284

conjunction

/kənˈdʒʌŋkʃn/ n. 链接；结合

| logical **conjunction** | 逻辑与（逻辑与是二元逻辑运算符，两个变量都为真时结果为真） |

Performs short-circuiting logical conjunction on two expressions.
对两个表达式执行简化逻辑合取。

derivative

/dɪˈrɪvətɪv/ n. 派生物，衍生物；派生词

second **derivative**	二阶导数
first **derivative**	一阶导数
partial **derivative**	偏导数
time **derivative**	时间导数
bounded **derivative**	有界导数

The first derivative of a state variable must appear in this study.
状态变量的一阶导数必须出现在这个研究中。

Day 285

engineer

/ˌendʒɪˈnɪə(r)/ n. 工程师；设计师

requirements **engineer**	需求工程师
performance **engineer**	运行性能分析工程师
knowledge **engineer**	知识工程师
traffic **engineer**	交通工程师；运输工程师
security **engineer**	安全工程师

This has been built together with domain experts and knowledge engineers.
这与领域专家和知识工程师共同建设。

flexibility

/ˌfleksəˈbɪləti/ *n.* 灵活性；弹性；柔性

response **flexibility**	响应灵活性
basic **flexibility**	基本灵活性
underlying **flexibility**	潜在灵活性

This approach reinforces the underlying flexibility of E2 by enabling users to select from a range of available models and methods for each step.
这一方法使得用户能够从每一步的模型和方法中做出选择，增强了 E2 的潜在灵活性。

Day 286

interactive

/ˌɪntərˈæktɪv/ *adj.* 交互式的；人机对话的；互动的

interactive learning	互动式学习
interactive video	互动视频；交互式视频
interactive search	互动搜索
interactive query	交互查询
interactive multimedia	交互式多媒体

Military and government use of interactive multimedia instruction has grown steadily.
军队和政府使用交互式多媒体的情况稳定增加。

robustness

/rəʊˈbʌstnəs/ *n.* 鲁棒性；稳健性；耐用性

system **robustness**	系统鲁棒性
noise **robustness**	噪声鲁棒性
improve **robustness**	提高鲁棒性
robustness analysis	鲁棒分析
robustness performance	鲁棒性性能

The new algorithm incorporates both robustness approaches and anchoring theories.
新算法同时包含鲁棒性方法和锚定理论。

Day 287

acceptance

/əkˈseptəns/ *n.* 接受；赞同，认可

social **acceptance**	社会认同
customer **acceptance**	客户验收；客户的接受程度
widespread **acceptance**	广泛接受
technology **acceptance**	技术接受
system **acceptance**	系统验收；制度承受

Both the initial system and its evolutions address the societal constraints critical to system acceptance and success.
初始系统和它的发展都涉及了对于系统接受度和成功至关重要的社会约束。

granularity

/ˌɡrænjəˈlærəti/ *n.* 间隔尺寸；粒度

suitable **granularity**	合适粒度
spatial **granularity**	空间粒度
server **granularity**	服务器粒度
intermediary **granularity**	中间粒度
influence **granularity**	影响粒度

A drawback of this approach is that it must be decided a priori what is the most suitable granularity.
这种方法的一个缺点就是必须事先决定最合适的粒度。

Day 288

average

/ˈævərɪdʒ/ *v.* 平均为，平均达到；计算平均值；将……平均分配

average out to	平均达到

We have assumed the noise terms average out to be small.
我们已经假设噪音均值很低。

accomplish

/əˈkʌmplɪʃ/ v. 完成；实现

accomplish the task	完成任务
accomplish the system	完成系统
accomplish the goal	完成目标
accomplish software development	完成软件开发

Our team accomplished software development.
我们的团队完成了软件开发。

Day 289

removal

/rɪˈmuːvl/ n. 清除；消除

malware removal	恶意软件清除
value removal	值删除
label removal	标签删除
stopword removal	停用词消除
noise removal	去噪

They processed a corpus with stopword removal, part-of-speech tagging and linguistic patterns selection.
他们对一个语料库进行了停用词去除、词性标注和语言特征选取。

fluid

/ˈfluːɪd/ adj. 流动的；液体的

fluid flow	流体流动
fluid dynamics	流体动力学

fluid particle	流体颗粒
fluid model	流体模型
fluid simulation	流体模拟,流体仿真

Since our method is based on the existing Fluid Model Solver (FMS), we compare our time-adaptive fluid solver (AFS) with the normal Fluid Solver (FS).
鉴于我们的方法以现有的流体模型求解器为基础,我们对比了实时自适应流体模型求解器和普通流体求解器。

Day 290

eigenvalue

/ˈaɪɡənˌvæljuː/ n. [数] 特征值

minimum **eigenvalue**	最小特征值
maximum **eigenvalue**	最大特征值
negative **eigenvalue**	负特征值
dominant **eigenvalue**	[数] 主本征值;主特征值
non-zero **eigenvalue**	非零特征值

The process we propose for selecting the maximum eigenvalue and the mass matrix is as follows.
我们提出的选择最大特征值和大容量矩阵的方法如下。

spectrum

/ˈspektrəm/ n. 范围,幅度;光谱

frequency **spectrum**	频率谱
problem **spectrum**	问题谱
broad **spectrum**	广谱
wide **spectrum**	广泛的范围
power **spectrum**	功率谱

The power spectrum is computed from a spatial average over the black box.
功率谱借助黑盒子的空间均值计算得来。

Day 291

comparable

/ˈkɒmpərəbl/ *adj.* 可比的,可比较的;类似的,同类的

comparable performance	可比较的表现
comparable sizes	可比较的大小
comparable results	可比较的结果
comparable evaluation	可比较的评价
comparable tool	可比较的工具

Due to its simplicity and comparable performance to more complex methods, the classification scheme that combines PCA and the Gaussian classifier outlined in Section 2.2.1 will be evaluated here.
这一分类方案与更复杂的方法相比更为简单,融合了主成分分析和2.2.1小节将会评价的高斯分频符。

configure

/kənˈfɪɡə(r)/ *v.* 安装,装配;(计算机)配置,设定

configure the feature	配置特性
configure the system	配置系统
configure the simulation	配置模拟
configure the database	配置数据库
configure the transformation	配置转变

We applied our tool to configure the feature model based on randomly generated preferences.
我们基于随机生成的偏好采用工具配置特征模型。

Day 292

simplicity

/sɪmˈplɪsəti/ *n.* 简单(性);容易(性)

computational **simplicity**	计算简单性
algorithmic **simplicity**	算法简单性
structural **simplicity**	结构简单性
syntactic **simplicity**	句法简单性
operational **simplicity**	操作简单性

The results show that with its operational simplicity, the self-repairing tree is able to provide a viable alternative to other proposals.
研究显示,自我修复树操作十分简单,能够为其他提案提供可替代方案。

precise
/prɪˈsaɪs/ *adj.* 精确的;准确的

precise information	准确信息
precise definition	准确定义
precise way	准确方式
precise quantitative method	准确量化方法
precise description	准确描述

Although the precise information about how the costs were accumulated from the children is lost, the total sum is available from the parent.
尽管我们缺失如何收集儿童成本的准确信息,然而我们仍然可以从父母那里获取总和。

Day 293

approximate
/əˈprɒksɪmət/ *adj.* 大概的;近似的

approximate solution	近似解决方案
approximate reasoning	近似推理
approximate path	近似路径
approximate entropy	近似熵
approximate value	近似值

This means that agents can find an approximate solution faster than the optimal one but still provide a theoretical guarantee.
这说明代理商可以找到一个比最优方案更快的近似解决方案,同时提供理论保证。

header

/ˈhedə(r)/ n. 标题

header file	头文件
header field	标题字段
packet header	数据包头部
request header	请求头
message header	消息头

The data structure shown in Fig. 3 contained header file and data arrays.
图 3 中的数据结构包含头文件和数据组。

Day 294

deformation

/ˌdiːfɔːˈmeɪʃn/ n. 变形

deformation gradient	[力]变形梯度
deformation kinematics	变形运动学
deformation mapping	变形映射
deformation response	变形响应
deformation simulation	变形模拟

Finally, we examine the stability, the size of the contribution of the lifting operator to the value of the deformation gradient.
最后,我们考察了稳定性和提升算子对于变形梯度值的贡献。

horizontal

/ˌhɒrɪˈzɒntl/ adj. 水平的

horizontal grid	水平栅格,水平网格
horizontal direction	水平方向
horizontal velocity	水平速度
horizontal row	水平排列
horizontal line	水平线

It is a poor choice for this example as near the surface the flow changes slower in the

horizontal direction than in the vertical.
这个案例的选择并不理想,因子水平方向流动变化比垂直方向缓慢。

Day 295

enforcement
/ɪnˈfɔːsmənt/ *n.* 实施;执行

law **enforcement**	法律执行
policy **enforcement**	政策执行
regulatory **enforcement**	监管执法;强制执法
hardware **enforcement**	硬件执行
technical **enforcement**	技术执行

From this it is shown that there is a theoretical and substantive basis for differentiation between management and technical enforcement roles in security.
由此可见,区分安全中的管理和技术执行具有理论和实质性基础。

desirable
/dɪˈzaɪərəbl/ *adj.* 令人向往的;值得拥有的;可取的

desirable features	理想特征
desirable solution	理想解决方案
desirable model	理想模型
desirable characteristics	理想特征
desirable behavior	理想行为

Importantly, we note that the modifications that we propose in this paper complement, the desirable features of ant-based routing algorithms.
重要的是,我们要注意本论文中提出的修订算法是蚁群路由算法理想特征的补充。

Day 296

terminate
/ˈtɜːmɪneɪt/ *v.* 终止;使……结束

terminate task	终止任务
terminate the process	终止过程
terminate the iterative process	终止迭代过程
terminate the application	终止应用
terminate the discovery process	终止发掘过程

"End" simply indicates that the server is unable to deliver any more answers; it is conventionally used to terminate the process of responding to a query.
"结束"此处暗示服务器无法给出更多答案,而"结束"传统上用于终止查询过程的回应。

timing

/ˈtaɪmɪŋ/ *n.* 时间;时机

timing information	时间信息
timing results	计时结果
timing channels	计时通道
timing attack	时序攻击
timing value	时间价值

When timing information is added to the specification of a Multi-Level Secure (MLS) system, it may reveal new information flow.
如果我们把时间信息加入多级安全系统描述,它可能会表现出新的信息流。

Day 297

plot

/plɒt/ *v.* 绘制;绘图

plot the solution	绘制解决方案
plot the results	绘制结果
plot the percentage	绘制百分比
plot the delay	绘制延迟
plot the value	绘制值

In Fig. 1 we plot the solution to the problem.
图1绘制了问题的解决方案。

tolerance

/ˈtɒlərəns/ *n.* 容忍

error **tolerance**	容错；误差宽容度
risk **tolerance**	风险承受能力
fault **tolerance**	容错性；指计算机系统或其他设备在出现故障时仍能继续运行的能力

We explored the efficiency and fault tolerance of search networks that have those properties.
我们探索了具备这些属性搜索网络的效率和容错性。

Day 298

split

/splɪt/ *v.* 分开；分裂

split into two parts	分裂为两部分
split into two groups	分裂为两组
split into varying numbers	分成不同数字
split into two stages	分成两个阶段
split into two categories	分成两组

After a short introduction into the used metrics, the evaluation will be split into two parts.
简要介绍过使用的度量后，评价将分为两部分。

reminder

/rɪˈmaɪndə(r)/ *n.* 提示信；通知单

speech **reminder**	语音提示
security **reminder**	安全提示
repeated **reminder**	重复提示
send **reminder**	发送提示

Thus it could be embarrassing to receive a speech reminder about medication while someone is visiting.
因此，当有人到访时收到服药语音提醒将会让人感到尴尬。

Day 299

manipulate
/məˈnɪpjuleɪt/ v. 操纵；摆布

manipulate the data	操纵数据
manipulate the model	操纵模型
manipulate the results	操纵结果
manipulate the properties	操纵属性
manipulate the path	操纵路径

Not validating the input allows a malicious user to directly manipulate the data returned by the database to obtain potentially sensitive information.
不验证输入使得恶意用户可以直接操纵数据库返回的数据，获得潜在敏感信息。

baseline
/ˈbeɪslaɪn/ n. 底线；基线

baseline case	基线案例
baseline system	基线系统
baseline scenario	基准情景
baseline model	基准模型
baseline algorithm	基线算法

The first evaluation compared the baseline system with ViGOR in order to assess ViGOR's grouping paradigm.
首次评估把基线系统和 ViGOR 放在一起比较，用于评估 ViGOR 的分组范式。

Day 300

biometric
/ˌbaɪəʊˈmetrɪk/ adj. 生物统计的；生物特征识别的

biometric system	生物识别系统
biometric data	生物特征数据

biometric authentication	生物特征认证
biometric sample	生物特征样本
biometric identification	生物识别

User authentication, biometric verification and biometric identification mechanisms address a diversity of Computer-Human Identification challenges.
用户认证、生物特征认证和生物特征识别机制处理了各式各样的人机识别挑战。

encoding
/ɪnˈkəʊdɪŋ/ n. 编码

correct encoding	正确编码
binary encoding	二进制编码
integer encoding	整数编码
dictionary encoding	词典编码
encoding algorithm	编码算法

Clearly, the variation of the average time is linear using integer or binary encoding process.
显然,平均时间的差异是线性的,中间涉及整数或二元编码。

总词汇表

model *n.*
system *n.*
data/datum *n.*
algorithm *n.*
network *n.*
set *n.*
node *n.*
process *n.*
base *v.*
function *n.*
security *n.*
application *n.*
level *n.*
type *n.*
parameter *n.*
set *v.*
table *n.*
path *n.*
image *n.*
query *n.*
domain *n.*
software *n.*
search *n.*
variable *n.*
element *n.*
graph *n.*
class *n.*
simulation *n.*
knowledge *n.*
source *n.*
task *n.*
pattern *n.*
web *n.*

resource *n.*
constraint *n.*
distribution *n.*
input *n.*
framework *n.*
instance *n.*
structure *n.*
error *n.*
probability *n.*
code *n.*
evaluation *n.*
model *v.*
compute *v.*
definition *n.*
edge *n.*
implementation *n.*
object *n.*
ontology *n.*
traffic *n.*
sequence *n.*
link *n.*
form *n.*
tree *n.*
message *n.*
vector *n.*
representation *n.*
interaction *n.*
select *v.*
range *n.*
matrix *n.*
cluster *n.*
language *n.*
classification *n.*

location *n.*
scheme *n.*
access *n.*
database *n.*
program *n.*
packet *n.*
document *n.*
operation *n.*
entity *n.*
environment *n.*
measure *v.*
optimal *adj.*
equation *n.*
accuracy *n.*
technology *n.*
address *v.*
device *n.*
detection *n.*
behavior/behaviour *n.*
complexity *n.*
output *n.*
semantic *adj.*
protocol *n.*
computational *adj.*
degree *n.*
accord *v.*
construct *v.*
global *adj.*
dataset *n.*
grid *n.*
boundary *n.*
standard *adj.*
procedure *n.*
list *n.*
server *n.*
key *adj.*
linear *adj.*
interface *n.*
threshold *n.*
category *n.*

iteration *n.*
length *n.*
aspect *n.*
failure *n.*
execution *n.*
process *v.*
architecture *n.*
theory *n.*
mapping *n.*
configuration *n.*
phase *n.*
enable *v.*
assign *v.*
organization *n.*
metric *n.*
argument *n.*
combination *n.*
mesh *n.*
spatial *adj.*
proof *n.*
assumption *n.*
cell *n.*
computation *n.*
approximation *n.*
operator *n.*
file *n.*
kernel *n.*
store *v.*
subset *n.*
memory *n.*
capability *n.*
cluster *v.*
variation *n.*
similarity *n.*
bug *n.*
choice *n.*
dimension *n.*
uncertainty *n.*
numerical *adj.*
request *n.*

extract *v.*
layer *n.*
extension *n.*
machine *n.*
characteristic *n.*
computer *n.*
finite *adj.*
dynamic *adj.*
profile *n.*
classifier *n.*
analyze *v.*
coefficient *n.*
form *v.*
developer *n.*
reference *n.*
attribute *n.*
correlation *n.*
map *n.*
vulnerability/vulnerabilities *n.*
physical *adj.*
Internet *n.*
prediction *n.*
processing *n.*
optimization *n.*
specification *n.*
equal *adj.*
frequency *n.*
cyber *adj.*
basic *adj.*
testing *n.*
engineering *n.*
experimental *adj.*
write *v.*
efficiency *n.*
correspond *v.*
statistical *adj.*
return *v.*
base *n.*
address *n.*
link *v.*

velocity *n.*
sensor *n.*
share *v.*
theorem *n.*
execute *v.*
core *n.*
update *v.*
constant *adj.*
hypothesis *n.*
label *n.*
capacity *n.*
infrastructure *n.*
expression *n.*
noise *n.*
pixel *n.*
client *n.*
formula *n.*
interval *n.*
storage *n.*
classify *v.*
topology *n.*
consistent *adj.*
transformation *n.*
density *n.*
estimation *n.*
map *v.*
validation *n.*
ratio *n.*
minimum *adj.*
bandwidth *n.*
concentration *n.*
underlie *v.*
calculation *n.*
formulation *n.*
curve *n.*
chain *n.*
block *n.*
online *adj.*
signature *n.*
partition *n.*

vertex *n.*
module *n.*
active *adj.*
setting *n.*
check *v.*
key *n.*
volume *n.*
interpretation *n.*
encode *v.*
dynamics *n.*
heuristic *adj.*
stream *n.*
channel *n.*
programming *n.*
cycle *n.*
reasoning *n.*
planning *n.*
bound *n.*
frame *n.*
refinement *n.*
functionality *n.*
logic *n.*
empirical *adj.*
label *v.*
minimize *v.*
platform *n.*
identification *n.*
transaction *n.*
deployment *n.*
temporal *adj.*
assignment *n.*
convergence *n.*
parallel *adj.*
effectiveness *n.*
inference *n.*
anomaly *n.*
query *v.*
monitor *v.*
filter *n.*
simulate *v.*

engine *n.*
filter *v.*
retrieval *n.*
static *adj.*
explicit *adj.*
mobile *adj.*
signal *n.*
access *v.*
annotation *n.*
verify *v.*
validity *n.*
symbol *n.*
virtual *adj.*
adapt *v.*
locate *v.*
update *n.*
verification *n.*
technical *adj.*
root *n.*
loop *n.*
adaptive *adj.*
scope *n.*
mode *n.*
likelihood *n.*
equivalent *adj.*
computing *n.*
allocation *n.*
valid *adj.*
center *n.*
learning *n.*
library *n.*
usage *n.*
utility *n.*
format *n.*
continuous *adj.*
automated *adj.*
hierarchy *n.*
binary *adj.*
triangle *n.*
precision *n.*

feedback *n.*
uniform *adj.*
segment *n.*
violation *n.*
depth *n.*
catchment *n.*
overlay *v.*
magnitude *n.*
aggregation *n.*
minimal *adj.*
projection *n.*
prototype *n.*
extraction *n.*
filtering *n.*
tagging *n.*
pseudo *adj.*
validate *v.*
malicious *adj.*
robot *n.*
deploy *v.*
evolution *n.*
discrete *adj.*
plot *n.*
highlight *v.*
monitoring *n.*
exact *adj.*
regression *n.*
Gaussian *adj.*
propagation *n.*
authorization *n.*
prior *adj.*
bound *v.*
read *v.*
retrieve *v.*
guarantee *v.*
eliminate *v.*
overview *n.*
probabilistic *adj.*
template *n.*
segmentation *n.*

list *v.*
robust *adj.*
theoretical *adj.*
appendix *n.*
priority *n.*
polynomial *adj.*
processor *n.*
integrated *adj.*
indicator *n.*
generic *adj.*
metadata *n.*
bias *n.*
code *v.*
generalize *v.*
structural *adj.*
scale *v.*
decomposition *n.*
availability *n.*
hybrid *adj.*
sampling *n.*
stable *adj.*
quantitative *adj.*
nonlinear *adj.*
Markov *n.*
modification *n.*
interpolation *n.*
notation *n.*
recall *n.*
diagram *n.*
calibration *n.*
track *v.*
email *n.*
implication *n.*
runtime *n.*
motivation *n.*
hierarchical *adj.*
metric *adj.*
manipulation *n.*
workflow *n.*
transmission *n.*

wireless n.
visual adj.
indices n.
consistency n.
integer n.
competitive adj.
fuel n.
agile adj.
flux n.
abstract adj.
paradigm n.
fraction n.
taxonomy n.
exceed v.
enforce v.
efficiently adv.
couple v.
infer v.
violate v.
abstraction n.
digital adj.
hardware n.
schema n.
character n.
logical adj.
implicit adj.
optimize v.
discovery n.
quantify v.
repository n.
identifier n.
manually adv.
exhibit v.
mathematical adj.
schedule n.
conditional adj.
buffer n.
trace n.
automatic adj.
normalize v.

collaboration n.
approximate v.
intermediate adj.
adoption n.
formulate v.
feasible adj.
hidden adj.
latency n.
adaptation n.
quantity n.
transfer n.
classical adj.
phenomenon n.
dependency n.
remote adj.
frequent adj.
core adj.
syntax n.
applicable adj.
transfer v.
maximum n.
motivate v.
default n.
switch v.
guideline n.
display v.
entropy n.
project v.
convert v.
translate v.
minimum n.
stochastic adj.
allocate v.
overlap v.
card n.
bit n.
iterative adj.
transmit v.
check n.
weighted adj.

content *adj.*
realistic *adj.*
connectivity *n.*
yield *n.*
operational *adj.*
delete *v.*
computationally *adv.*
translation *n.*
diffusion *n.*
portion *n.*
displacement *n.*
recovery *n.*
count *n.*
maximize *v.*
enterprise *n.*
fusion *n.*
histogram *n.*
propagate *v.*
respective *adj.*
collaborative *adj.*
trigger *v.*
gradient *n.*
correspondence *n.*
independently *adv.*
accurately *adv.*
constrain *v.*
synthetic *adj.*
sequential *adj.*
matching *n.*
structured *adj.*
coarse *adj.*
polygon *n.*
formally *adv.*
preprocessing *n.*
target *v.*
compromise *v.*
setup *n.*
span *v.*
visualization *n.*
modified *adj.*

generator *n.*
simultaneously *adv.*
flexible *adj.*
electronic *adj.*
outlier *n.*
array *n.*
annotate *v.*
positive *adj.*
predictor *n.*
log *n.*
compute *n.*
analytical *adj.*
composition *n.*
systematic *adj.*
recover *v.*
legitimate *adj.*
detector *n.*
alignment *n.*
peer *n.*
request *v.*
return *n.*
versus *prep.*
scalability *n.*
align *v.*
sort *v.*
snapshot *n.*
separately *adv.*
endpoint *n.*
video *adj.*
safety *n.*
assertion *n.*
vertical *adj.*
discharge *n.*
equilibrium *n.*
corpus *n.*
battery *n.*
expectation *n.*
estimator *n.*
relational *adj.*
port *n.*

extensive *adj.*
principal *adj.*
quadrature *n.*
meaningful *adj.*
block *v.*
fit *n.*
increment *n.*
artifact *n.*
numerous *adj.*
carrier *n.*
rotation *n.*
straightforward *adj.*
manifold *n.*
exception *n.*
maintenance *n.*
forwarding *n.*
insert *v.*
representative *adj.*
command *n.*
load *v.*
conjunction *n.*
derivative *n.*
engineer *n.*
flexibility *n.*
interactive *adj.*
robustness *n.*
acceptance *n.*

granularity *n.*
average *v.*
accomplish *v.*
removal *n.*
fluid *adj.*
eigenvalue *n.*
spectrum *n.*
comparable *adj.*
configure *v.*
simplicity *n.*
precise *adj.*
approximate *adj.*
header *n.*
deformation *n.*
horizontal *adj.*
enforcement *n.*
desirable *adj.*
terminate *v.*
timing *n.*
plot *v.*
tolerance *n.*
split *v.*
remainder *n.*
manipulate *v.*
baseline *n.*
biometric *adj.*
encoding *n.*

参 考 文 献

[1] BREZINA V, MCENERY T, WATTAM S. Collocations in context: A new perspective on collocation networks [J]. International Journal of Corpus Linguistics, 2015, 20(2): 139-173.

[2] COXHEAD A. A new academic word list [J]. TESOL Quarterly, 2000, 34(2): 213-238.

[3] GARDNER D, DAVIES M. A new academic vocabulary list [J]. Applied Linguistics, 2014, 35(3): 305-327.

[4] LEI L, LIU D. A new medical academic word list: A corpus-based study with enhanced methodology [J]. Journal of English for Academic Purposes, 2016(22): 42-53.

[5] NATION ISP. Making and using word lists for language learning and testing [M]. 3rd ed. Amsterdam, Netherlands: John Benjamins Publishing Company, 2016.

[6] WEST M. A general service list of English words [M]. London, New York: Longman, Green, 1953.